Howard Brenton

NEVER SO GOOD

NICK HERN BOOKS
London
www.nickhernbooks.co.uk

A Nick Hern Book

Never So Good first published in Great Britain as a paperback original in 2008
by Nick Hern Books Limited, 14 Larden Road, London W3 7ST

Never So Good copyright © 2008 Howard Brenton

Howard Brenton has asserted his right to be identified as the author of this work

The sketch from *Beyond the Fringe* is reproduced by kind permission of the
Estate of Peter Cook

Cover image: Harold Macmillan making a speech in Brighton,
October 1957. © Hulton-Deutsch Collection/Corbis
Cover design: Ned Hoste, 2H

Typeset by Nick Hern Books, London
Printed and bound in Great Britain by CPI Bookmarque, Croydon, CR0 4TD

A CIP catalogue record for this book is available from the British Library

ISBN   978 1 85459 551 5

Mixed Sources
Product group from well-managed
forests and recycled wood or fiber
www.fsc.org Cert no. TT-COC-002227
© 1996 Forest Stewardship Council
FSC

HOWARD BRENTON

Howard Brenton was born in Portsmouth in 1942. His many
plays include *Christie in Love* (Portable Theatre, 1969);
Revenge (Theatre Upstairs, 1969); *Magnificence* (Royal Court
Theatre, 1973); *The Churchill Play* (Nottingham Playhouse,
1974, and twice revived by the RSC, 1978 and 1988); *Bloody
Poetry* (Foco Novo, 1984, and Royal Court Theatre, 1987);
Weapons of Happiness (National Theatre, Evening Standard
Award, 1976); *Epsom Downs* (Joint Stock Theatre, 1977); *Sore
Throats* (RSC, 1978); *The Romans in Britain* (National Theatre,
1980); *Thirteenth Night* (RSC, 1981); *The Genius* (1983),
Greenland (1988) and *Berlin Bertie* (1992), all presented by the
Royal Court; *Kit's Play* (RADA Jerwood Theatre, 2000); *Paul*
(National Theatre, 2005) and *In Extremis* (Shakespeare's Globe,
2006 and 2007).

Collaborations with other writers include *A Short Sharp Shock*
(with Tony Howard, Royal Court and Stratford East, 1980);
Pravda (with David Hare, National Theatre, Evening Standard
Award, 1985); *Iranian Nights* (with Tariq Ali, Royal Court
Theatre, 1989); *Moscow Gold* (with Tariq Ali, RSC, 1990); *Ugly
Rumours* (with Tariq Ali, Tricycle Theatre, 1998); *Collateral
Damage* (Tricycle Theatre, 1999) and *Snogging Ken* (Almeida
Theatre, 2000), both with Tariq Ali and Andy de la Tour.

He wrote the libretto for Ben Mason's football opera *Playing
Away* (Opera North and Munich Biennale, 1994) and a radio
play, *Nasser's Eden* (1998). Versions of classics include *The
Life of Galileo* (1980) and *Danton's Death* (1982) both for the
National Theatre, and Goethe's *Faust* (1995/6) for the RSC.

His novel *Diving for Pearls* was published by Nick Hern Books
in 1989. His book of essays on the theatre, *Hot Irons*, was
published by Nick Hern Books (1995) and reissued, in an
expanded paperback version, by Methuen (1998). He wrote
thirteen episodes of the BBC1 drama series *Spooks* (2001- 2005,
BAFT

Other Titles in this Series

Never So Good was first performed in the Lyttelton auditorium of the National Theatre, London, on 26 March 2008 (previews from 17 March), with the following cast:

HAROLD MACMILLAN	Jeremy Irons
YOUNG HAROLD MACMILLAN	Pip Carter
NELLIE MACMILLAN	Anna Carteret
DOROTHY MACMILLAN	Anna Chancellor
RONALD KNOX	Tim Frances
YOUNG HARRY CROOKSHANK	Ben Addis
HARRY CROOKSHANK	Terence Wilton
WINSTON CHURCHILL	Ian McNeice
ANTHONY EDEN	Anthony Calf
SELWYN LLOYD	Peter Forbes
ROBERT 'BOB' BOOTHBY	Robert Glenister
SERGEANT ROBINSON	Nicholas Lumley
NEVILLE CHAMBERLAIN	Terrence Hardiman
DWIGHT D EISENHOWER	Clive Francis
SMITHSON	Jonathan Battersby

ENSEMBLE   Sarah Head, Sioned Jones, Anne Kavanagh, Charlotte Melia, Roger Ringrose, Janet Spencer-Turner, Claire Winsper, Rupert Young

Director   Howard Davies
Designer   Vicki Mortimer
Lighting Designer   Mark Henderson
Music   Dominic Muldowney
Choreographer   Lynne Page
Sound Designer   Paul Arditti

NEVER SO GOOD

Howard Brenton

To Jane

Characters

HAROLD MACMILLAN
YOUNG HAROLD MACMILLAN
HELEN 'NELLIE' MACMILLAN, *his mother*
DOROTHY MACMILLAN, *his wife*
RONALD KNOX
YOUNG HARRY CROOKSHANK
HARRY CROOKSHANK
WINSTON CHURCHILL
ANTHONY EDEN
SELWYN LLOYD
ROBERT 'BOB' BOOTHBY
NEVILLE CHAMBERLAIN
DWIGHT D. EISENHOWER
SERGEANT ROBINSON

SMITHSON, *a servant*
AMERICAN LIEUTENANT
BUTLER
1ST SOLDIER
2ND SOLDIER
3RD SOLDIER

Also: Eton Wall Game players, a company of dancers, soldiers, staff at Downing Street, servants, Eisenhower's aides, waiters, marines, security men, press men, film crew, crowds

This play went to press before the end of rehearsals and so may differ slightly from the play as performed.

ACT ONE

The Wound (1909-1916)

HAROLD MACMILLAN *wanders onto the stage. White tie, an elegant cane in one hand, a whisky and soda in the other. He is very relaxed and addresses the audience.*

MACMILLAN. I always had trouble with my teeth. Bad teeth in politics are not good. It's cruel, but people will always make moral judgements from appearances. It got a lot worse when television came. The BBC was a dental nightmare.

He sips his whisky.

Enter the Eton Wall Game. Two teams of eleven young PLAYERS *in pre-First World War games kit. Amongst them are the* YOUNG HAROLD MACMILLAN *and* YOUNG HARRY CROOKSHANK.

As they enter they are singing the Eton Boating Song, raucously:

PLAYERS. Jolly boating weather,
    And a hay harvest breeze,
    Blade on the feather,
    Shade off the trees,
    Swing swing together,
    With your bodies between your knees,
    Swing swing together,
    With your bodies between your knees.

The PLAYERS *jam in a huddle against the wall.*

They shout:

YOUNG CROOKSHANK. Bully! Bully! Bully! Bully! Bully! Bully!

They freeze.

MACMILLAN (*aside*). Winston always had good teeth. Despite the cigars, Cuban tobacco juices flowing in the root canals. It was probably the brandy kept the Churchillian enamel clean. When I became Prime Minister I had my errant incisors capped. I also grew my hair thicker, oiled it a little. And when I went to Moscow to meet the Communist leaders, I wore a furry, white Russian hat. Yes, in politics one learns to play the tart.

The Wall Game continues. One team – the Collegers – are struggling to form a phalanx, a tunnel at an angle to the wall.

YOUNG CROOKSHANK (*shouting*). College! College! Phalanx! Phalanx! College, phalanx!

The Wall Game freezes.

MACMILLAN (*aside*). Chipped a tooth in the Eton Wall Game. The rules allow a fist to be held permanently in the face of an opponent without actually punching them – a very English kind of brutality. Thoroughly enjoyed playing the Wall Game. Every century or so someone actually scores a goal. Which is meant to teach one something, though I haven't the faintest idea what.

The Wall Game continues.

YOUNG MACMILLAN *breaks away from the mass of bodies. The ball flies out to him. He is startled to find it in his hands.*

YOUNG CROOKSHANK. Harold! Lines! Kick! Lines!

YOUNG MAC *kicks the ball offstage. The other* PLAYERS *rush off shouting:*

PLAYERS. Calyx calyx calyx! Ball in bad calyx! Well done, Harold! Ball in calyx!

YOUNG MAC *and* MACMILLAN *pause. Then they talk to each other.*

YOUNG MAC. I hated Eton.

MACMILLAN. That's why I draw a veil.

YOUNG MAC. When Mummy took me out of college, they said I'd been sent away for buggery.

MACMILLAN. Draw a veil.

YOUNG MAC. Mummy told people it was pneumonia.

MACMILLAN. Yes.

YOUNG MAC *and* MACMILLAN *both take out rimless glasses, put them on and look at each other.*

Then YOUNG MAC *runs off.*

MACMILLAN *smiles at the audience.*

(*Aside.*) Anthony Eden. Anthony had wonderful teeth, a dazzling array for the television age. But not even that beautiful mouth in millions of living rooms could save him. And teeth weren't my biggest physical problem. That began in the Great War. When my mother finally got me there.

Enter HELEN 'NELLIE' MACMILLAN. *She paces. She reads a letter. She folds it into her hand.*

Enter YOUNG MAC. *He is in the civilian day clothes of 1915.*

NELLIE. Harold, darling boy.

Kisses him.

Were you very late last night?

YOUNG MAC. Very.

NELLIE. How is Southend?

YOUNG MAC. Beastly.

NELLIE. But lots of sea air.

YOUNG MAC. Oh, billows and billows.

NELLIE. Well, that will do you good...

YOUNG MAC. To be stuck in the Royal Rifle Corps, and in Southend-on-Sea! It's too bloody shaming.

NELLIE. You've been ill, Harold.

YOUNG MAC. The war to save civilisation breaks out and I get appendicitis! And put in a training battalion, where the only dangerous thing is a portion of fish and chips! Somehow, one way or another, I've just got to try to get shot.

NELLIE. No, Harold.

YOUNG MAC. Well, shot at. You do want me to fight, don't you?

NELLIE. Of course I want you to fight! But I also think of what it means.

YOUNG MAC. It means glory.

NELLIE. Or vanity.

YOUNG MAC. Not... not... not if it's glory in the eye of God.

She sighs.

NELLIE. Oh, Harold, you can be so serious, sometimes it makes my skin crawl.

YOUNG MAC. Oh. Very sorry.

NELLIE. It's just that when you were a boy I wish you had... sometimes, you know, done things with frogs.

YOUNG MAC. What things with frogs? Pulled their legs off?

NELLIE. Well, yes.

YOUNG MAC. Amazing the ways one can disappoint one's mother.

NELLIE. If you ever really disappointed me, Harold, you'd know it.

YOUNG MAC. Yes. I think I would.

They laugh. They kiss cheeks.

NELLIE. I've done a thing.

YOUNG MAC. What thing?

NELLIE. Don't go cranky on me.

YOUNG MAC. What have you done?

NELLIE. Cranky, serious on me.

YOUNG MAC. Mummy... what?

NELLIE. I have, how to say this... I have prostituted my
position in English society on your behalf. Well, at least,
cashed my position in. I've got you a commission in the
Grenadier Guards.

A beat.

YOUNG MAC. That's a shocking thing to do.

NELLIE. I know.

SMITHSON, *a servant, is approaching. With great respect
he carries before him, on a hanger, the uniform of a Captain
of the Grenadier Guards.*

YOUNG MAC. Privilege of the worst kind.

NELLIE. I know.

YOUNG MAC. Really shocking!

NELLIE. Yes.

YOUNG MAC. And absolutely, tremendously wonderful.

NELLIE *is delighted.*

He sees SMITHSON *with the uniform.*

Oh, Smithson, I say.

A nod from NELLIE *to* SMITHSON.

SMITHSON. Perhaps, sir, you would like to change into the
uniform of an officer and a gentleman?

NELLIE *turns her back on them.* YOUNG MAC, *with*
SMITHSON's *help, begins to change into the uniform.*

YOUNG MAC. The only privilege I'm taking is, I suppose, to
get myself killed or wounded as soon as possible.

NELLIE. One thing I want you to promise: you won't see
Ronald Knox before you go.

MACMILLAN. Never leaves you, that nursery taste in the
mouth. The late-night, 'be a good boy', 'mother knows best'
kiss. So warm and smothering.

YOUNG MAC. I should see him...

NELLIE. Harold, listen to me. Never be dependent on men like that.

YOUNG MAC. He was a brilliant teacher for me, after Eton. And he was wonderful at Oxford...

NELLIE. I hated him being there with you.

YOUNG MAC. He was so hurt when you fired him as my tutor. I think he had a spiritual crisis.

NELLIE. We are not on earth to have spiritual crises. We're here to do God's will. And make the best of ourselves.

YOUNG MAC. I never said, but I was hurt too.

He has not finished dressing, but NELLIE *turns on him.*

NELLIE. I thought Ronald Knox's relationship with you was... unhealthy.

YOUNG MAC *laughs.*

YOUNG MAC. You mean you thought we were buggers?

SMITHSON *looks away.*

NELLIE. That's not a proper word to use afront of me.

YOUNG MAC. Dreadfully sorry, Mummy, I didn't mean to...

NELLIE. He nearly got you, Harold. Be honest. He nearly had you kissing the Pope's ass.

SMITHSON *looks away again.*

YOUNG MAC. Mother, proper word...?

She smiles, then persists.

NELLIE. But a Roman Catholic in England will never be able to have high office under the Crown. Never... be a Government minister.

YOUNG MAC *finds this ludicrous and laughs.*

YOUNG MAC. That's ridiculous. Who ever said I want to be a Government minister! After the war I'll... be a publisher,

like Father. Or a traveller, or an explorer. I don't know what
I'll be.

NELLIE. Just don't see Ronald. Don't be dependent on
anyone.

YOUNG MAC. Not even on you?

NELLIE. That's different, I'm your mother.

They smile.

Then she is serious.

You will always win through in the end. That's why you had
to go to Eton and go on to Oxford. That's why you must do
this. Because you will win through.

She kisses him, sweeps away and exits.

MACMILLAN *finishes changing into the Guards uniform.*

SMITHSON. What shall I pack, sir?

YOUNG MAC. Oh, I think... just the Bible. And a Greek
Testament.

MACMILLAN. And *The Imitation of Christ.* St Augustine.
Boethius's *Consolation.*

YOUNG MAC. Homer's *Iliad* – in the Greek. And Aeschylus.

MACMILLAN. Theocritus. Horace.

YOUNG MAC. Shakespeare's *Henry IV. Twelfth Night. The
Winter's Tale* Meredith

MACMILLAN. Browning's *The Ring and the Book.* Ruskin's
Sesame and Lilies and *Crown of Wild Olive.*

YOUNG MAC. And anything by Trollope.

SMITHSON. Yes, sir.

Distant bugles call.

St James's Park.

YOUNG MAC *is waiting for someone.*

MACMILLAN (*aside*). None of us knew what we were doing, of course. To us at the beginning of the Great War, the world was a ripening peach, and we were eating it. And looking back, how lovely we were, and so earnest, and innocent.

Enter RONALD KNOX. *He is dressed in High Anglican priest's garb. He is taken aback for a moment by* YOUNG MAC's *uniform.*

YOUNG MAC. Ronnie.

KNOX. Harold, dearest.

They embrace.

St James's Park. The place for assignations of high state.

YOUNG MAC. Hardly what this is.

KNOX. Could be an assignation of the high Spirit?

YOUNG MAC. You can't mean alcohol.

KNOX. Could mean both. Anglicanism has many inhibitions but at least it's not against drink. (*Re: the uniform.*) Grenadier Guards?

YOUNG MAC. Yes. The 4th Battalion.

KNOX. 4th?

YOUNG MAC. They're a newly formed unit. Active.

KNOX. You're going to fight.

YOUNG MAC. Absolutely.

KNOX. And I thought you were safe with a bucket and spade, in a regiment no one had heard of.

YOUNG MAC. No longer. I'm a bomb officer. I've been training my men. Not that we've actually got any bombs.

KNOX. You will have. Harold...

YOUNG MAC. We've been stationed at Marlow. It's been like a perpetual garden party. Can't wait for the reality.

KNOX. And when do you leave the 'unreal' for the 'real'?

YOUNG MAC. On Thursday.

KNOX is shocked.

KNOX. And that's what you wanted to tell me?

YOUNG MAC. In a way.

KNOX. 'In a way.' I've decided to go over.

A beat.

I'm going to convert.

A beat.

Harold, at last, I'm going to Pope!

YOUNG MAC. Ah.

This is a Macmillan 'Ah'. It signals a massive betrayal. He uses it only at crucial moments in his life.

KNOX. God is leading me home.

YOUNG MAC. But you took orders as an Anglican priest! Balliol College have made you their chaplain. What are they going to say?

KNOX. Oh, there'll be a lot of shouting over the port about Papist plots. But none of that matters. I've done what we dreamed of.

YOUNG MAC. I'm not coming with you. I can't Pope.

A beat.

KNOX. I knew it. When I saw you just now, coming towards me, looking around you.

YOUNG MAC. What, you mean in a shifty Protestant manner?

KNOX. Yes, actually. You are shifty.

YOUNG MAC. Ronnie, I owe you so much. My whole brain is in a whirl. God's going to have not to mind. I know I'm lagging and timid, but I can't do the Roman Catholic performance now...

KNOX. You're gushing. Do me the courtesy of not gushing.

YOUNG MAC. I am horribly sorry.

A beat.

KNOX. I'm not going to let you get away with this. At Oxford you were so hot for conversion. Your passion, your religious fervour, I thought: 'Dear God, one day this man may be a cardinal.'

YOUNG MAC. Yes, the Roman fever.

This is an insulting phrase used by Anglicans about Roman Catholicism. It angers KNOX.

KNOX. Why, Harold?

YOUNG MAC. I've been thinking of my people.

KNOX. You mean your mother.

YOUNG MAC. The British people, actually. I don't want to cut myself off from them. From what they know.

KNOX. That stinks! That's narrow nationalism! After the war, men will look to two institutions beyond the boundaries of country: International Socialism and the Roman Catholic Church.

YOUNG MAC. If I'm a Catholic I'll...

KNOX. What, never be in the Cabinet?

YOUNG MAC. I don't know, I... after this war I think I'll have to just relearn everything.

KNOX. Don't let her win.

A beat.

Pray with me.

YOUNG MAC *looks around.*

YOUNG MAC. In the middle of St James's Park...

KNOX. Jesu will lead you.

YOUNG MAC. Ronnie...

KNOX. Kneel down on the grass with me, now, right here.

YOUNG MAC. Ronnie, don't make a scene.

KNOX *grabs* YOUNG MAC'*s hands*.

KNOX. Harold, imagine us, you and I, stepping out on the steps of St Peter's, arm in arm before the great Square, having just had the Pope's blessing. Privately... We could arrange that, you know, with our connections. That day can happen, my dear. I beg you. Reconsider.

YOUNG CROOKSHANK, *also in the uniform of the Grenadier Guards, has entered. He strides cheerfully up to* KNOX *and* YOUNG MAC.

YOUNG CROOKSHANK. Harold, there you are. I thought you said near the flamingos.

YOUNG MAC. We walked on a bit. Ronnie, this is Harry Crookshank. We're in the same battalion. Harry, this is Ronald Knox.

KNOX. Pleased to meet you... is it Captain Crookshank?

YOUNG CROOKSHANK. Same rank as Harold. Jolly, isn't it? Very pleased to meet you, Father.

KNOX. Not quite Father yet...

YOUNG MAC. Come on, Ronnie, be flattered.

YOUNG CROOKSHANK. Well, lunch is it? The Ritz?

KNOX (*low, to* YOUNG MAC). You arranged to meet him?

YOUNG MAC (*low*). Yes.

KNOX (*low*). To cut me short...

YOUNG MAC (*low*). Ronnie...

KNOX (*low*). Low cunning. I've not seen that before. There some kind of politician in you?

YOUNG MAC (*low*). I don't know what's in me.

YOUNG CROOKSHANK. Er... Chaps...

YOUNG MAC. Ronnie, come and have lunch with us.

KNOX. I don't think so.

YOUNG CROOKSHANK. Oh, do. Priests aren't out of place in the Ritz. Now the war's on, it's rather like the last of days in there.

KNOX. I enjoy the Ritz, but not today. Gentlemen. I'll pray for you when you're in France. Goodbye, Harold.

YOUNG MAC. Goodbye, Ronnie.

KNOX *strides away, without shaking hands, and exits.*

YOUNG CROOKSHANK. So that's the man who meant so much to you.

YOUNG MAC. Yes.

YOUNG CROOKSHANK. Odd cove. Come on, champers!

MACMILLAN. What did we think at the beginning of the war? We thought: dance! Dance to Flanders.

They exit.

MACMILLAN *is still on the stage.*

Enter DANCERS *at the Ritz. They are dancing a ballroom tango.* YOUNG MAC *and* YOUNG CROOKSHANK *join them. Gaiety, laughter.*

Bugles begin to clash with the music of the dance. They become louder and louder. The dance begins to disintegrate.

An explosion.

Gas drifts.

Enter BRITISH SOLDIERS *in First World War battle kit – struggling to pull on gas masks, two of them shouting:*

SOLDIERS. Gas! Gas! Gas! Gas!

One of them throws gas masks to YOUNG MAC *and* YOUNG CROOKSHANK.

The DANCERS *scatter and exit.*

MACMILLAN (*aside*). I always had difficulty with gas masks, getting them on over my glasses.

Explosions.

YOUNG MAC *and* YOUNG CROOKSHANK *run, doubled over, as if through trenches. They reach a command post.*

They sit slumped, out of breath, at an extreme of exhaustion.

In the far distance, a man is screaming.

After a while the scream stops.

They take off their gas masks.

YOUNG CROOKSHANK. Is this Piccadilly?

YOUNG MAC. I think it's Hyde Park Corner.

YOUNG CROOKSHANK. Didn't recognise it.

YOUNG MAC. Probably because it's a hole dug in mud.

YOUNG CROOKSHANK. If we're at Hyde Park Corner, we're two hundred yards off position.

YOUNG MAC. The company will bunch up.

YOUNG MAC *takes out a notebook and a pencil.*

YOUNG CROOKSHANK. This constant battlefield thing of not knowing where the blind blazes you are.

YOUNG MAC. Athena sent a mist.

YOUNG CROOKSHANK. What?

YOUNG MAC. In the Trojan War. The goddess Athena was always sending down a mist. Mind you, it wasn't chlorine gas.

YOUNG CROOKSHANK. The stuff back there, it was ours, wasn't it? We pulled back and got caught in our own gas.

YOUNG MAC *writes.*

MACMILLAN (*aside*). 'Dear Mummy, the flies on the Somme are again a terrible plague, and the stench from the dead bodies which lie in heaps around us is awful.'

YOUNG CROOKSHANK. Couldn't they see we were pulling back? It's a bloody disgrace.

YOUNG MAC. We gas ourselves, the Boche gas themselves. It all evens up.

YOUNG CROOKSHANK. Odd thing to say, Harold.

YOUNG MAC. Not at all. In the end there is a scheme of things.

YOUNG CROOKSHANK. Really? What?

YOUNG MAC. I hang on to the British Empire. That all this is worthwhile, for the British Empire. That's the glory.

YOUNG CROOKSHANK *closes his eyes, exhausted.*

YOUNG MAC *writes.*

MACMILLAN (*aside*). 'And Mummy, no, a steel vest would be of no use. Nor would earmuffs keep out the noise.'

SERGEANT ROBINSON *enters running, doubled over. He goes into the command post.*

YOUNG CROOKSHANK. Sergeant Robinson. Thank God.

SERGEANT. Captain Macmillan, sir; Captain Crookshank, sir.

YOUNG CROOKSHANK. Are we at Hyde Park?

SERGEANT. Piccadilly, sir.

YOUNG CROOKSHANK. Piccadilly after all…

SERGEANT. Yes, sir.

YOUNG MAC. Is the company in good order?

SERGEANT. Best as can be expected, sir.

YOUNG MAC. I'd better see my bombardiers…

SERGEANT. I suggest when they're rested up… sir.

YOUNG MAC. You're right. I'll inspect in the morning, an hour before the push.

SERGEANT. How about a brew, gentlemen?

YOUNG CROOKSHANK. Very cosy of you, Sergeant. Tea for two.

YOUNG MAC. And a plate of cucumber sandwiches.

YOUNG CROOKSHANK. Egg and cress for me.

The three of them laugh.

YOUNG MAC *takes out a book and begins to read.*

SERGEANT. Er… there is a bottle.

They are very interested.

YOUNG CROOKSHANK. Bottle?

YOUNG MAC. Bottle of what?

SERGEANT. Brandy, sir.

YOUNG CROOKSHANK. Not that Frog village hooch that
blinded three bombardiers…

SERGEANT. Napoleon 1884, actually, sir. From the chateau at
Bray.

YOUNG CROOKSHANK. I thought Colonel Carter was sitting
on that.

SERGEANT. Not since this morning, sir.

YOUNG CROOKSHANK. Ah. Well. A bottle would be very
jolly.

SERGEANT. Thank you, sir.

He exits.

YOUNG MAC. Bring out your dead and their brandy.

YOUNG CROOKSHANK. You're getting very acerbic these
days, Harold.

YOUNG MAC. Am I? Dreadfully sorry. I must try harder to fail
to impress.

YOUNG CROOKSHANK *looks at* YOUNG MAC, *who
reads on.*

YOUNG CROOKSHANK. Homer again?

YOUNG MAC. Yes.

YOUNG CROOKSHANK. Trojan War. Magnificently bloody show, from what I do remember. Do you read it to make you fierce?

YOUNG MAC. More to keep me civilised. Harry, after the war, let's refuse to do things.

YOUNG CROOKSHANK. How do you mean?

YOUNG MAC. Start... a league of individuals.

YOUNG CROOKSHANK. What, some kind of political party?

YOUNG MAC. More a group. We'll all go to live in Italy. In a villa with cypresses. And drink the Italian wines, with their dear names.

Enter SERGEANT ROBINSON. *He has tin mugs, a bottle of brandy and a buff-brown envelope.*

YOUNG CROOKSHANK. Ah, excellent, forget tea at the Ritz.

SERGEANT. Orders from Brigade, sir.

YOUNG MAC. Thank you very much, Sergeant. (*Opening the envelope.*) Do have some brandy.

SERGEANT. Thank you, sir.

A moment.

YOUNG MAC *reads the orders.*

YOUNG CROOKSHANK *pours brandy then hands the bottle to the* SERGEANT.

Forgive manners, sir.

YOUNG CROOKSHANK. Please.

The SERGEANT *swigs from the bottle.*

YOUNG MAC. Sergeant, the battalion's orders for tomorrow are to advance on the machine-gun emplacement at Ginchy. Close to Delville Wood.

The three of them are shocked.

YOUNG CROOKSHANK. Tall order.

SERGEANT. The Boche machine gunners on our flank, the lot that gave us the trouble today, sir. Do we clear them out first?

YOUNG MAC. No, we are to advance on Ginchy as quickly as we can. We go at six twenty hours.

SERGEANT. Yes, sir.

YOUNG MAC. Goodnight, Sergeant.

SERGEANT. Goodnight, sir. Goodnight, sir.

MACMILLAN (*aside*). Routine before an advance. Stuff pockets with cigarettes. Check pistol ammunition. Check morphine shots. Have a great big whack of any alcohol around.

Bombardment. It is very loud.

YOUNG MAC *and* YOUNG CROOKSHANK *take big swigs from the bottle of brandy. They take out their pistols.*

Whistles are being blown.

YOUNG MAC *leads* SERGEANT ROBINSON *and* SOLDIERS *toward the German line – i.e. upstage.*

YOUNG CROOKSHANK *veers away.*

Terrifying noise. They shout.

YOUNG MAC. Sergeant Robinson!

SERGEANT. Captain Macmillan, sir!

YOUNG MAC. Are we at brown?

SERGEANT. Blue, I think, sir!

YOUNG MAC. Can't be blue, we're not past green!

SERGEANT. Deploy into line, sir?

YOUNG MAC. Yes, yes, deploy into line!

SERGEANT. Line! Line!

The SERGEANT *blows his whistle.*

A second's silence. Everyone is still.

And suddenly everyone on the stage sings:

ALL. Blade on the feather
     Shade off the trees…

A second's silence. All still.

A shot.

YOUNG MAC *falls.*

The war effects return.

SERGEANT. Are you hit, sir!?

YOUNG MAC. Take the men on in line!

SERGEANT. But you're hit, sir!

YOUNG MAC. Take the men on!

SERGEANT. Come back for you, sir!

YOUNG MAC. Take them on!

The SERGEANT *blows a whistle. He leads the* SOLDIERS *upstage.*

The war effects stop. All except MACMILLAN *freeze.*

MACMILLAN (*aside*). These were the five wounds I received
in the First World War. To the head, at the Battle of Loos, on
the 27th of September, 1915: a glancing shot. Incredibly
lucky. Concussed. Lost on the battlefield. Tried to dig in.
Second wound later that day, in the right hand. Fractured third
metacarpal bone. Excruciating pain. Troubled me for the rest
of my life – flabby handshake, always a political drawback.
Decades later, someone called Peter Cook was to mock me
for it. Then, on the Somme, 13th of July, 1916. Third wound.
Again, head. Lost my glasses this time. 15th September,
1916, still on the Somme, the big push to Ginchy. Fourth
wound, knee. Kept going. Then – shot in the left buttock.
Bullet in pelvis. Managed to roll into a foxhole. Dosed myself
with morphine. Lay there. Eight hours. Read Aeschylus.

YOUNG MAC *has taken out a small leather-bound volume.
He reads aloud.*

YOUNG MAC. '*Agamemnonos se phem epoopsesthai moron.*'

A beat.

'*Agamemnonos se phem epoopsesthai moron.*'

A beat.

'*Agamemnonos se phem epoopsesthai moron.*'

MACMILLAN. 'I say you shall look upon Agamemnon dead.'

YOUNG MAC. 'I say you shall look upon Agamemnon...'

He is still.

SERGEANT ROBINSON, *with two* SOLDIERS *who pull a stretcher, crawls towards* YOUNG MAC.

SERGEANT. Captain Macmillan, can you hear me? Captain Macmillan?

YOUNG MAC *turns his head and looks at him.*

Permission to move you, sir.

YOUNG MAC. Yes, about time you did, I'd have thought, Sergeant.

SERGEANT. Did you take a shot of morphine, sir?

YOUNG MAC. Could do with a brandy.

SERGEANT (*low*). Orderly. (*Loud.*) Right, lads, careful as you can.

A SOLDIER *gives* YOUNG MAC *a shot. They put a blanket over him. Lift him and carry him.*

After a few steps they freeze. YOUNG MAC *addresses* MACMILLAN *from the stretcher.*

YOUNG MAC. It's the guilt!

MACMILLAN *turns on* YOUNG MAC.

MACMILLAN. Enough!

They are glaring at each other.

A beat.

YOUNG MAC (*simultaneously*). I should have died –

MACMILLAN (*simultaneously*). I should have died in the war.

YOUNG MAC. Instead I'm dead in you...

MACMILLAN. I had those two summers, Oxford before the
war...

YOUNG MAC. Punt on the river, sunlight across a parasol...
tosh. An opened French window onto a dappled lawn in
endless summer, all tosh, tosh the endless dribble of old men
going on about the war I didn't die in...

MACMILLAN. But I did take one thing from the Guards. A
sense of a thing done beautifully well.

YOUNG MAC. Tosh, tosh, tosh...

MACMILLAN (*aside*). That and the suffering of the working-
class soldier. The soldiers in the mud, the generals in their
French chateaus. That too.

YOUNG MAC. It's a lie, you lied to yourself, you all did, all of
you, lied.

A beat. They look at each other.

MACMILLAN. You've dogged me all these years...

YOUNG MAC. Woof woof.

MACMILLAN. Will you ever leave me alone?

YOUNG MAC. Oh, yes.

Unspoken answer: 'When we die.'

A beat.

Then the SERGEANT *and the two* SOLDIERS *run with*
YOUNG MAC *on the stretcher. They put him down and
run off.*

Two other SOLDIERS *run on, carrying* YOUNG
CROOKSHANK *on a stretcher. He is put down beside*
YOUNG MAC. *He is covered in blood. The* SOLDIERS
run off.

Harry.

YOUNG CROOKSHANK. Harold.

YOUNG MAC. I've got it in the rump. What about you?

YOUNG CROOKSHANK. Me? All shot away. Down there. Wedding tackle.

YOUNG MAC. Harry, my dear chap...

YOUNG CROOKSHANK. Shot my fucking balls off!

Two SOLDIERS *run on and lift* YOUNG CROOKSHANK *on his stretcher.*

At the same time, NELLIE *enters pushing a wheelchair.*

Castrato! Me! What shall I do, sing in opera like some... squealing pig, piggy-piggy, squealy piggy...

As he is carried off on the stretcher, YOUNG CROOKSHANK *cries out, high squealing sounds.*

At the same time, NELLIE *helps* YOUNG MAC – *the blanket held around him – into the wheelchair.*

YOUNG MAC (*aside*). Eight of us in my year, 1912. Eight scholars, Balliol College, Oxford.

MACMILLAN (*aside*). After the war, I thought: 'Make a difference.'

YOUNG MAC (*aside*). Eight young men. We all went to fight.

MACMILLAN (*aside*). Thought: 'Make the world a better place.'

YOUNG MAC (*aside*). Only two of us came back. Of my year. Two.

NELLIE *is wheeling* YOUNG MAC *away.*

MACMILLAN (*aside*). Tradition does not mean that the living are dead, it means that the dead are living.

YOUNG MAC *laughs and waves as* NELLIE *wheels him away.*

And I did. Despite the hand, the leg. And the teeth. I did do something. I did.

End of Act One.

ACT TWO

Churchill's Dogs (1938-1943)

Heston Aerodrome, 30th September, 1938.

NEVILLE CHAMBERLAIN *addresses a crowd of* PRESS
MEN *with cameras, a* FILM CREW *with a camera and
recording devices, and various* WELCOMERS. *He has a piece
of paper in his hand.*

CHAMBERLAIN. This morning I had another talk with the
German Chancellor, Herr Hitler, and here is the paper that
bears his name upon it as well as mine.

*He waves the paper to the crowd, to loud cheers and 'Hear,
hear's.*

My good friends, a British Prime Minister has returned from
Germany bringing peace with honour. I believe it is peace
for our time.

Loud cheers.

Exit CHAMBERLAIN *and the scene at the aerodrome.*

*The garden on the Macmillans' family home in Cadogan
Square.*

Enter HAROLD MACMILLAN. *He is now 44 years old. He
has yet to acquire the pomp of his 'elder statesman' self. He
is dressed in white tie.*

YOUNG MAC *enters.* MACMILLAN *turns on him.*

MACMILLAN. What are you doing here?

YOUNG MAC. The same as you. To see if she's dead.

MACMILLAN (*to* DOROTHY). Darling, thank you so much
for...

DOROTHY. No no, Harold...

MACMILLAN. I came the minute I...

DOROTHY. Dearest, don't worry, it's all right.

MACMILLAN. Is it?

DOROTHY. She's much better.

MACMILLAN. Really?

A beat.

You know, I thought this time...

DOROTHY. She suddenly perked up and got out of bed.

MACMILLAN. Thank God.

DOROTHY. No, don't thank Him. Thank Neville Chamberlain.

MACMILLAN. What?

DOROTHY. When she heard the news from Munich she just
threw the bedclothes off and called for Smithson.

MACMILLAN. I see.

DOROTHY. *Et voilà.*

A now-decrepit SMITHSON *enters, pushing* NELLIE *in a
wheelchair. She is wrapped up, a blanket over her knees. A
watchful* NURSE *follows.*

NELLIE. Harold, dearest.

DOROTHY. I'll leave you.

MACMILLAN (*sotto, to* DOROTHY). Don't you dare. (*To*
NELLIE.) Mummy.

NELLIE. Well, now all your nonsense can stop.

MACMILLAN. What nonsense is that, Mother dear?

NELLIE. Don't patronise me, Harold, just because I'm dying.

DOROTHY (*to* MACMILLAN). I'll stay.

MACMILLAN (*to* DOROTHY). Bless you.

NELLIE. Now Neville's got us peace, you can join his
Government.

MACMILLAN. I don't think Neville will have me.

NELLIE. He will if you break with Churchill.

A beat.

MACMILLAN. Mummy, talking with you about Winston always ends badly.

NELLIE. And you know why! I've gotten ill watching you, wrecking your career. First there was Stockton.

MACMILLAN. Mummy, not Stockton too...

NELLIE. It's full of poor voters. In awful clothes. Those horrible caps.

MACMILLAN. Their clothes and their poverty are hardly their fault...

NELLIE. I blame you, Dorothy.

DOROTHY. Oh, really?

NELLIE. I'm sure they saw through Harold. But you dazzled them.

DOROTHY. True, they did tend to throw their horrible caps in the air when I was around.

DOROTHY *smiles at* MACMILLAN.

MACMILLAN. I did get elected.

NELLIE. But spouting crackpot Communist ideas on a soapbox in Stockton streets had nothing to do with it. It was your wife's legs in silk stockings standing next to you.

MACMILLAN. What do you mean, 'Communist ideas'...?

NELLIE. That dreadful book you've written. *The Middle Way*, what does that mean? How can anything be 'middle'? Things are one thing or the other, right or wrong.

MACMILLAN. A middle way: mixed economy, minimum wage, nationalise gas and coal...

NELLIE. Yes, yes, go ahead, stick onion domes on top of the House of Commons and call it the Kremlin, why not?

DOROTHY *laughs*. MACMILLAN *is not amused*.

Oh, Harold, why did you have to get a constituency north of Watford? Why not somewhere with your own kind, like... Bromley.

MACMILLAN. It may be regrettable, but there is another 'kind' living in this country...

DOROTHY *touches his arm*.

DOROTHY. Pointless...

NELLIE. And then this opposition to all of dear Neville's attempts to make peace. Sneering and sniping on the backbenches with Winston Churchill and his cronies.

MACMILLAN. I can't go on fighting with you about Winston...

NELLIE. Yes you can! The man's a goddamn drunk!

MACMILLAN. He has principles.

NELLIE. Principles out of a brandy glass.

MACMILLAN. We can't trust Hitler.

NELLIE. He's signed an agreement.

MACMILLAN. It means nothing.

NELLIE. He's just another politician.

MACMILLAN. He is not.

NELLIE. I don't know why you're all so down on Mr Hitler. People I know who've met him say he's charming. He's apparently rather hairy about the wrists, but that's no reason to accuse him of everything under the sun.

MACMILLAN *is angry*.

MACMILLAN. That's just typical house-party, cocktail-driven nonsense! I'd have thought you'd be beyond that, Mother.

DOROTHY. Nellie, I think perhaps...

NELLIE (*to* MACMILLAN). You were always, always easily led. There was that Popish homosexual.

MACMILLAN. I don't think Ronnie...

NELLIE. Had to tear you from his clutches.

MACMILLAN (*to* DOROTHY). Help.

DOROTHY (*to* MACMILLAN). No way out.

NELLIE. Now it's Churchill.

DOROTHY (*to* NELLIE). I don't think Winston goes both ways...

NELLIE. Always led! Like that Eton thing.

DOROTHY looks at MACMILLAN. She does not know what NELLIE means.

MACMILLAN. Mother, go back to bed.

A beat.

NELLIE. You'll never be it, you know.

MACMILLAN. Be what?

NELLIE. It.

She gestures to SMITHSON. He wheels her away. They and the NURSE exit.

DOROTHY. What 'Eton thing'?

MACMILLAN. I've no idea.

DOROTHY does know.

DOROTHY. You always told me you left Eton because of pneumonia.

MACMILLAN. Well, that's what she must have meant.

A beat.

DOROTHY. Why are you dressed up?

MACMILLAN. I'm going on to supper at the Ritz, with Winston.

DOROTHY. Before the debate in the House.

MACMILLAN. Yes.

DOROTHY. Conspirators all.

MACMILLAN. Absolutely.

He looks at his watch.

I must put my best foot forward...

DOROTHY. Will Bob Boothby be there?

MACMILLAN. Yes, of course.

DOROTHY. Winston relies on him a lot.

MACMILLAN. Bob's very able. Darling, cheek...

DOROTHY *offers a cheek, he pecks a kiss and turns to go.*

DOROTHY. Bob and I sleep together.

MACMILLAN *freezes.*

We have for a long time, actually.

A beat.

A very long time. Yes, we have had a very long affair. And are still having it. Right under your nose, your stupid nose.

A beat.

I'm not saying sorry. Awful of me not to, I know. But I don't feel guilty. I can't explain it. Yes I can. It makes me feel alive. That's why I have no choice, you see, I must feel alive. Bloody selfish really, for Godsake say something!

MACMILLAN. I know.

A beat.

DOROTHY. Know?

MACMILLAN. About you and Bob.

DOROTHY. You know?

MACMILLAN. Oh, yes.

DOROTHY. Don't put on your silly, silly grin.

MACMILLAN. It's not a grin. It's just surprise at the world.
    The damn awful world.

DOROTHY. Oh, Harold. Harold, do you know what you are? A klutz.

MACMILLAN. What is a klutz?

DOROTHY. It doesn't matter...

MACMILLAN. No, please tell me. One must rely on an unfaithful wife for something. Even if it's only for keeping up with the slang of the dance halls.

DOROTHY. Maybe you aren't a klutz. Maybe you're a cold-hearted bastard.

MACMILLAN. No, I'm not that. If I were, I'd be what my mother calls 'It'. By which I think she means 'someone with power'. Perhaps I should try to be a cold-hearted bastard...

DOROTHY. Don't, Harold...

MACMILLAN. ... Really try. Then I could do something, hit you, isn't that what cold-hearted bastards do? Hit their wives?

DOROTHY. At least they fuck them.

They stare at each other.

A beat.

Often. More often. More than...

A beat.

MACMILLAN. Yes, well, I must get to the Ritz...

DOROTHY. For Godsake, talk to me!

MACMILLAN. There is a crisis in the country.

DOROTHY. Yes, and if you and Winston are right and bombs are going to fall, isn't now the time to be honest? All dance, fall into each other's arms before the Nazis goose-step down Whitehall?

MACMILLAN. That is what we are trying to stop.

DOROTHY. Falling into each other's arms?

MACMILLAN. You're being flippant, Dorothy, please stop it, you are better than this. This is an hour of maximum danger.

DOROTHY. Oh, poo-poo-poo... Yes, the 'hour of maximum danger', but isn't now exactly the time when we could... decide to live differently? Can't we change ourselves?

MACMILLAN. I think in this world we have the selves we are stuck with. Unfortunately.

A beat.

DOROTHY. How long have you known?

MACMILLAN. Since 1931.

DOROTHY. 19... seven years?

MACMILLAN. Yes.

DOROTHY. Since when you...

MACMILLAN. Were in hospital in Switzerland, yes.

DOROTHY. You mean your breakdown was something to do with Bob and me?

MACMILLAN. What do you think?

DOROTHY. You never said.

MACMILLAN. Well, if you remember, I could hardly say anything at all. That's why a nervous breakdown is something of a handicap for a politician.

DOROTHY. I did come to Switzerland.

MACMILLAN. Then went back to London. Seeking comfort.

DOROTHY. I'm not with Bob for comfort.

A beat.

MACMILLAN. I am going to be terribly late. One must always keep abreast of the intake of alcohol with Winston. Particularly if one is discussing the end of civilisation...

He turns to go but she holds his arm, pulling him back.

DOROTHY. Please, just one more moment. One more. So we can be honest.

He takes her hand from him, and steps back.

MACMILLAN. Honest? There's nothing honest about us, how can there be? I am in a state of lying cuckolddom. Pretending that all is right with the world, while all the world knows about my marriage. In circles where I'm not a laughing stock, I'm pitied. I don't know which is worse.

DOROTHY. Well, if that's your state, what's mine? Sin?

A beat.

Oh. Oh. That's what you think, don't you? I'm in a state of sin.

MACMILLAN. That's not for me to say...

DOROTHY. It's still in there, isn't it? Under your skin. In your veins. Like some... disease your body will never get rid of. Your damn Catholicism.

MACMILLAN. Nonsense.

DOROTHY. Then give me a divorce.

The Macmillan 'Ah'...

MACMILLAN. Ah.

DOROTHY. Divorce me.

MACMILLAN. Do you want a divorce?

DOROTHY. I'm asking for one.

MACMILLAN. But do you really want one?

DOROTHY. For Godsake, you stuffed shirt, divorce me!

A beat.

MACMILLAN. No.

A beat.

DOROTHY. Why not?

MACMILLAN. It could make it impossible for me to hold any

high office. Or at the very least make it difficult.

DOROTHY. That's the reason?

MACMILLAN. I am a politician.

DOROTHY. Ambition?

MACMILLAN. 'That last infirmity of noble mind.'

DOROTHY. Bloody Milton?

MACMILLAN. Bloody Milton.

DOROTHY. You're a liar. It's not political ambition. You won't divorce me because God says you can't. Or the Pope says you can't. Or the Archbishop of Canterbury or some damn thing inside your head says you can't.

MACMILLAN. I do think... I do think we have to struggle along with what we're given.

DOROTHY. And you were given me.

MACMILLAN. Actually, we gave ourselves to each other, remember?

DOROTHY (*near tears*). Oh shoots, shoots.

She recovers.

I don't want a divorce either. You're not a laughing stock, Harold. On the contrary. You don't realise it, but we dazzle. People are amazed at the way we stay together, operate together. All eyes on us, when we enter a room? We, my darling, are the great political marriage of our day.

MACMILLAN. Are we?

DOROTHY. Well, perhaps not quite yet. But we could be.

MACMILLAN. So we carry on?

DOROTHY. Can you?

MACMILLAN. What is the choice?

DOROTHY. You could kick Bob's head in.

MACMILLAN. I suppose I could.

DOROTHY. Blackball him in your clubs. He'd hate that.

MACMILLAN. Yes.

DOROTHY. Well then.

MACMILLAN. Be a bit like shooting a fellow officer just as you go over the top together.

DOROTHY. And we can't have that, can we.

MACMILLAN. We'll carry on. As we are. 'I both hate and love, knowing not which is which.'

DOROTHY. Who said that?

MACMILLAN. Catullus.

DOROTHY. Ah. Well. Bully for Catullus. I won't be able to stop hurting you, you know.

MACMILLAN. No.

A beat.

I think Winston may ask me to go and see Neville, privately. Do you think I should?

DOROTHY. Yes.

MACMILLAN. It could sink me, once and for all.

DOROTHY. Do it. Because it's right.

MACMILLAN. Yes.

She goes to him and kisses him on the mouth. Then turns away. She laughs.

DOROTHY. Bob took me to a boxing match in the East End. It was very bloody. But very... manly.

MACMILLAN. I expect it was. Goodnight, Dorothy.

For a moment DOROTHY hesitates. Then they exit.

DANCERS at the Ritz enter.

Dance routine: a quickstep.

The DANCERS exit, passing WINSTON CHURCHILL as he

enters. He is in white tie, hunched, concentrated, cigar alight.

A WAITER *enters with a small table, a bottle of champagne in a bucket and an ashtray upon it. As he sets it down,* CHURCHILL *arrives. He is 64 years old. He pours himself a glass of champagne and drinks.*

MACMILLAN *enters.* CHURCHILL *does not see him.*

CHURCHILL (*mumbling*). Unmitigated... Equilibrium deranged... 'Art weighed in the balance...' ... moral health.

He sips again. He takes notes from his inside pocket. He looks at them, puts them back.

Then he launches, full-throated, into a rehearsal of a speech.

MACMILLAN *stands at the back behind him, listening.*

We have suffered a total and unmitigated defeat. You will find that in a period of time which may be measured by years, but may be measured by months, Czechoslovakia will be engulfed in the Nazi regime. We are in the presence of a disaster of the first magnitude... we have sustained a defeat without a war, the consequences of which will travel far with us along our road... we have passed an awful milestone in our history, when the whole equilibrium of Europe has been deranged, and that the terrible words have for the time being been pronounced against the Western democracies: 'Thou art weighed in the balance and found wanting.' And do not suppose that this is the end. This is only the beginning of the reckoning. This is only the first sip, the first foretaste of a bitter cup that will be proffered to us year by year unless by a supreme recovery of moral health and martial vigour, we arise again and take our stand for freedom as in the olden time.

MACMILLAN. Magnificent.

CHURCHILL. Oh, Harold. Caught with my rhetorical pants down.

He laughs.

Drink?

MACMILLAN. Please. I always thought you spoke off-the-cuff.

CHURCHILL (*pouring a glass for him*). Good God, no. In politics, spontaneity is far too important to be left to chance.

MACMILLAN. Is Neville going to make a statement to the House tonight?

CHURCHILL. Yes. And there'll be a division.

MACMILLAN. Well, when they hear what you're going to say, the House will move against him.

CHURCHILL. You don't for a minute believe that.

MACMILLAN. I want to.

CHURCHILL. Face reality. Neville Chamberlain is the most popular man in the country. They will cheer him to the roof. Peace is a heady opium.

MACMILLAN. What is Neville thinking of?

CHURCHILL. Oh, I can understand his thinking. He's feeding a crocodile, in the hope it will eat him last.

MACMILLAN. I've always thought he's a nice man.

CHURCHILL. God protect us from nice men.

MACMILLAN. But he's too middle class. Very, very narrow in view.

CHURCHILL. Everyone has his day. And some days last longer than others.

MACMILLAN. I must admit... when I heard him announce peace on the radio, I thought: 'Now my son will go to Oxford.'

CHURCHILL. I thought: 'Now my son will be a guerrilla fighting the Nazis in the Cotswold Hills.'

A beat.

MACMILLAN. Perhaps things are more up in the air...

CHURCHILL. Oh, the contrary, Harold. War is certain. And probably defeat.

MACMILLAN. And down below they're dancing, because they

think they're safe. It's fragile, isn't it? The state. The England we know. So fragile.

CHURCHILL. Yes.

A beat.

You have it too, don't you?

MACMILLAN. What do you mean?

CHURCHILL. The black dog.

MACMILLAN. No, that was... personal problems, I recovered.

CHURCHILL. It's not a weakness in a leader, Harold. It's a strength. The control of despair.

Enter BOB BOOTHBY. *He is overweight and 38 years old. He is quick and concerned.*

BOOTHBY. Winston, I telephoned his office but his PPS doesn't know where he is. Hello, Harold.

MACMILLAN. Good evening, Bob.

YOUNG MAC. That's the man who fucks your wife.

BOOTHBY. Did you all hear Neville?

MACMILLAN. Yes. He was irritatingly good.

BOOTHBY. I missed the damn thing.

MACMILLAN. Pity.

CHURCHILL. Telephone Anthony again, would you? It's vital he be here.

BOOTHBY. You know what Anthony's like.

CHURCHILL. 'Trailing clouds of glamour so we come.'

CHURCHILL *laughs*.

BOOTHBY. What?

MACMILLAN. Wordsworth. More or less.

BOOTHBY. I'll telephone again.

YOUNG MAC. He fucks your wife.

Exit BOOTHBY.

CHURCHILL. Bob was my Parliamentary Secretary, when I was Chancellor in '28.

MACMILLAN. Yes.

A beat.

CHURCHILL. Bob is immensely able.

MACMILLAN. Yes.

CHURCHILL. With some able people, you have to put a cordon sanitaire around their personal habits.

MACMILLAN. Personal habits.

YOUNG MAC. Like fucking your wife.

CHURCHILL. The next weeks and months are going to be very stressful. We who know what must be done with these gangsters in Berlin must keep together. The country depends on us... though it may not know it yet!

MACMILLAN. I appreciate what you say, Winston.

CHURCHILL (*low*). You could just take a mistress, you know.

MACMILLAN. I don't think so.

CHURCHILL. No? Well.

Enter ANTHONY EDEN. *He is 41 years old. He is wearing an opera cloak.*

The group assembles. They revolve around the pouring of champagne.

EDEN. Good evening.

CHURCHILL. Anthony, we've been telephoning you...

EDEN. I went round to see Diana Cooper.

CHURCHILL. Diana, why?

EDEN. You've not heard? Duff's resigned from the Admiralty.

CHURCHILL. Oh, that is so very brave.

MACMILLAN. You'd expect nothing else from him.

EDEN. He did it the moment Neville spoke on the wireless about his piece of paper.

CHURCHILL. Wasn't Duff with Diana?

EDEN. No. His first port of call will be...

A nod.

CHURCHILL. Oh, right.

YOUNG MAC. Duff Cooper, mistresses on trees.

MACMILLAN. How was Diana?

EDEN. Horribly upset. You know how she loves the ministerial life – the glittering place settings.

CHURCHILL. I'll telephone him. He must join we happy dissenters, with our bows and arrows in this political Sherwood Forest.

MACMILLAN. Otherwise known as the Ritz...

A WAITER *enters and approaches with a new bottle of champagne in a bucket.*

CHURCHILL. Did I order that?

WAITER. No, sir, but on account of peace in our time there's a run on the '08. I cornered a bottle for you.

CHURCHILL. Thoughtful of you, Bernard.

WAITER. Thank you, sir.

The WAITER *goes. Then they speak.*

EDEN. Are we all caught in a great delusion?

CHURCHILL. It is a fragile screen of complacency and self-deception, skilfully designed to delude a whole people. 'Peace in our time' is a very potent phrase. It's what people crave, no wonder they're celebrating. We, on the other hand, drink to steady our nerves.

They smile grimly.

Any other ministers stepping up to the block?

EDEN. It looks like Duff is the only one.

MACMILLAN. What of Walter Elliot, Oliver Stanley, Malcolm MacDonald...

EDEN. None of them.

CHURCHILL. They're frightened. Neville can be very vengeful.

EDEN. I could have given cover to Duff, by resigning too.

CHURCHILL. If you hadn't already resigned six months ago over Mussolini. Wrong dictator, perhaps?

CHURCHILL *winks at* MACMILLAN, *who smiles.* EDEN *does not realise he is being teased.*

EDEN. Yes, going over Munich would have made a bigger splash. But Neville was obsessed with making a private deal with Mussolini! Going behind my back...

CHURCHILL. You were absolutely right in what you did.

BOOTHBY *enters. He sees* EDEN.

BOOTHBY. Oh, you're here.

YOUNG MAC. Those little podgy hands, what have they touched?

CHURCHILL. Anthony, thank you for coming. I know your own group will have their views – 'the glamour boys', as the press have taken to calling you...

EDEN (*good humour*). Well, you have your dogs, Winston...

CHURCHILL (*good humour*). But there're not many of us in the party who oppose Neville's policy towards the Nazis. We must make sure we are all in step, if we are to avert disaster.

EDEN. The question is, what do we do in the Munich debate? I think we all vote against the Government. Let Neville withdraw the whip, even chuck us out of the party.

CHURCHILL. All of us here would do that...

MACMILLAN. Yes.

BOOTHBY. Yes.

CHURCHILL. ... But I think it better that we abstain.

EDEN. Won't that make us look awful namby-pambies?

CHURCHILL. It will look very well. We will sit for all to see on the Commons benches, while they all go to vote. And everyone will have to not look us in the eye. We must make our points in the debate against the Munich Agreement. But above all, what we must avoid is Neville calling a general election.

A beat.

MACMILLAN. Dear God, yes!

BOOTHBY. Don't get it.

MACMILLAN. We're in rebellion against our own party.

EDEN. Yes. On this wave of 'peace in our time', he could go to the country and wipe us out.

CHURCHILL. That's why we must revolt against his Government, but not quite succeed. Yet. I also think we should send an emissary.

BOOTHBY. To say what?

CHURCHILL. To put the case for a Government of National Unity.

EDEN *and* BOOTHBY *scoff.*

BOOTHBY. I cannot see Neville giving that the time of day...

CHURCHILL. No. But we will have to begin to speak of national unity and strength.

MACMILLAN. Not really our rhetoric.

CHURCHILL. We will get used to it.

EDEN. Well, who's going to go? If I walked up to Number Ten, Neville would have the constable on the door arrest me.

BOOTHBY. I'll do it.

CHURCHILL. I think someone with a little less baggage?

They all look at MACMILLAN.

CHURCHILL *and* BOOTHBY *exit.*

Enter the Cabinet Table. CHAMBERLAIN *is sitting at it.*

Enter MACMILLAN.

CHAMBERLAIN. Harold.

MACMILLAN. Good evening, Prime Minister.

CHAMBERLAIN. We must both be at the House in a few minutes so... come on, out with it. What's Winston sent you to say?

MACMILLAN. As a matter of courtesy, Prime Minister, I have to tell you a number of us are going to abstain tonight.

CHAMBERLAIN. Yes, fifteen is the Chief Whip's latest count. Anything else?

MACMILLAN. We think that you should consider a Government of National Unity.

CHAMBERLAIN (*laughs*). Oh, Harold, what are you doing?

MACMILLAN. I'm sorry?

CHAMBERLAIN. Running with Churchill's dogs. Leave that monster in his drinking den in the Ritz.

MACMILLAN. Prime Minister, I...

CHAMBERLAIN. I read your book.

A beat.

MACMILLAN. I'm flattered...

CHAMBERLAIN. We agree about so much. Look what I've begun. Decent women's pay in my Factory Act, slum clearance in my Housing Act. I don't go as far as nationalising the mines, as you do in your book, but my Coal Act's halfway there. And that's all in two years. We're both radical conservatives. We believe in the state as a guardian, setting decent living conditions so people can prosper, according to their talents. Winston is a diehard reactionary, any radicalism from his Liberal days long gone. You don't belong with him, you belong with me.

MACMILLAN. Perhaps. If we were in a time of peace.

CHAMBERLAIN. We are in a time of peace, I have secured peace.

MACMILLAN. Prime Minister, with respect, you...

CHAMBERLAIN. Shut up.

MACMILLAN. I...

CHAMBERLAIN. Shut up! I have won the peace. And Winston and his ragbag of warmongers will never come to power. I'm very sorry for you, you're a talented man, but there we are.

MACMILLAN. Thank you, Prime Minister.

CHAMBERLAIN. There will be no war.

MACMILLAN *walks away upstage*. CHURCHILL, SELWYN LLOYD, EDEN, HARRY CROOKSHANK, BOOTHBY *and various others enter*. MACMILLAN *joins them and they wait*.

...A SERVANT *puts a BBC microphone on the Cabinet Table.*

I am speaking to you from the Cabinet Room at 10 Downing Street. This morning the British Ambassador in Berlin handed the German Government a final note stating that unless we heard from them by eleven a.m. that they were prepared at once to withdraw from Poland, a state of war would exist between us. I have to tell you that no such undertaking has been received, and that consequently this country is at war with Germany. You can imagine what a bitter blow it is to me that all my long struggle to win peace has failed.

He stands.

The Cabinet Table swings away and off the stage.

The CROWD *around* CHURCHILL *bursts into applause. Some shake him by the hand, some slap him on the back.*

CHAMBERLAIN, *shuffling, walks towards the group.*

A silence.

CHURCHILL *steps forward and shakes* CHAMBERLAIN *by the hand. No applause, only embarrassment.*

CHAMBERLAIN *walks upstage through the* CROWD *and exits.*

They again cheer and applaud and sweep downstage.

WAITERS *appear, distributing champagne.*

CHURCHILL. This is the last Pol champagne from the sadly depleted stocks of Number Ten. But we will despair about nothing.

Laughter. He raises his glass.

To the utter confusion of our enemies and to victory!

ALL. Victory!

DANCERS, *both male and female, enter in wartime uniforms. They dance the jitterbug.*

All exit except for MACMILLAN, *and at the back* YOUNG MAC.

An AMERICAN LIEUTENANT *enters quickly.*

YOUNG MAC. Algiers, North Africa? What is this, Harold? A political Siberia, with sand?

LIEUTENANT. Mr Macmillan, sir. General Eisenhower needs to speak to you before you leave.

MACMILLAN. Where is he? I don't think I can leave the airfield...

LIEUTENANT. He's driving over here now.

MACMILLAN. Thank you, Lieutenant. Perhaps you could let the pilot of my plane know.

LIEUTENANT. Yes, sir.

He exits.

YOUNG MAC. Never near, never near, what what what will get you to 'It'? Will you know 'It' when you see it? Or has it gone already, the great chance for 'It'?

MACMILLAN *looks at his watch.*

MACMILLAN. Damn, damn.

YOUNG MAC. Damn, damn. Years of failure. Years of second string. Years of being the pinky-faced moustache with glasses, on the edge of the photographs of the famous meetings of the great. Churchill and Roosevelt in Casablanca? Who's that beanpole with the tash, leaning, back of Churchill's right shoulder, a kind of vacant grin?

MACMILLAN. This is a damn important job. Resident Minister, North Africa. Winston relies on me.

YOUNG MAC. Lies on you, fat Winston swinging in his favourite hammock, Harold the hammock...

MACMILLAN. The Joint Command of the Anglo-American North African Force is a great achievement. Operation Torch.

YOUNG MAC. But not lit by you – by Churchill, Eden, Roosevelt. The greats. You've achieved nothing. I'm dead in you for nothing. Why do you keep me in you? I'm dead, don't you know? I died. But you carry me round. In a sack. Called You. A sack called You. A sack called You.

MACMILLAN. Be quiet.

YOUNG MAC. Oooh, standing by an airfield in Africa, talking to yourself? Why don't you bury me in the sand? Get rid of me. Live. Like your wife and her lover...

MACMILLAN. Damn...

YOUNG MAC. Join them, you're a famous *ménage a trois*, why not, surprise them both in bed, fuck them, murder them, do something to be famous! Live!

Enter DWIGHT D. EISENHOWER *in military uniform.*

EISENHOWER. Harold, sorry to delay your flight.

MACMILLAN. Good evening, sir.

EISENHOWER. Jesus, why are you tuxed up?

MACMILLAN. Going directly to General de Gaulle's HQ for dinner.

EISENHOWER. Observing the niceties.

MACMILLAN. You have to with the General.

EISENHOWER. The hell don't you.

MACMILLAN. He can be rather grand.

EISENHOWER. It'll be nightfall before you reach Casablanca. You know there are sandstorm warnings.

MACMILLAN. I have to see de Gaulle. To discuss the deployment of his Free French forces.

EISENHOWER. Ah yes, well, that's what I want to talk to you about. Look, there are some – Robert Murphy one of them – who think we should break with the General.

MACMILLAN. I think that is a bad idea.

EISENHOWER. Murphy's Roosevelt's personal envoy.

MACMILLAN. De Gaulle is what we have.

EISENHOWER. The man is impossible.

MACMILLAN. He is in an impossible situation. An emperor without an empire.

EISENHOWER. That's certainly how he behaves. Murphy wants to replace him.

MACMILLAN. Who with?

EISENHOWER. General Clemont?

MACMILLAN. A nonentity, the French don't know him. At least de Gaulle is a very conspicuous flagpole for the French to rally round.

EISENHOWER. Well. Winston's put a good man out here in the sand.

MACMILLAN. Thank you.

EISENHOWER. I'll go with de Gaulle. Slap Murphy down. We've got boys fighting in the desert out here and we spend hours with this politicking.

MACMILLAN. At least things have livened up out here.

EISENHOWER. Hell yes. Six months ago the only political question in Cairo was is Diana Cooper going to sleep with our ambassador.

MACMILLAN. Absolutely.

EISENHOWER. Did she, by the way?

MACMILLAN. Er... I believe so.

EISENHOWER. Fly safe. Crack open a bottle when you're back.

MACMILLAN. Thank you, sir.

EISENHOWER *exits*.

(*Aside*.) The pilot of the plane was a charming Australian. Bit of a gum-chewer. And inexperienced. There was a sandstorm. Perfectly possible to fly above, but I experienced one of the really boring things about wartime diplomacy. An aircrash.

A very loud explosion. A stage effect of an aircrash. Debris falls.

Screaming, YOUNG MAC *helps* MACMILLAN *drag a* PILOT, *who is covered in blood, from the wreckage.* MACMILLAN's *dinner clothes are wrecked, torn and covered in blood.*

The three figures lie on the stage.

YOUNG MAC. Harold.

MACMILLAN. Yes.

YOUNG MAC. You saved the pilot.

MACMILLAN. Yes.

YOUNG MAC. You know how to do this.

MACMILLAN. Yes.

YOUNG MAC. You nearly died once before.

MACMILLAN. Yes.

YOUNG MAC. Last war, now this war...

MACMILLAN. Yes...

YOUNG MAC. So near to death, yet you survive...

MACMILLAN. Yes.

YOUNG MAC. Survive for what? To always be on the edge, decent but dull, nice man but mousy, brilliant but always second best?

A beat.

MACMILLAN. Survive for 'It'.

YOUNG MAC. Change, be at the centre...

MACMILLAN. ... 'It'...

YOUNG MAC. ... be decent, but deceive...

MACMILLAN. ... 'It'...

YOUNG MAC. ... nice man, but a knife within...

MACMILLAN. ... 'It'...

YOUNG MAC. ... brilliant, but better than anyone else...

MACMILLAN. 'It'... 'Power'.

YOUNG MAC. Promise me! Now!

MACMILLAN. I promise myself.

Both still, as if dead.

End of Act Two.

Interval.

ACT THREE

The Suez Betrayal (1956)

A field near Chartwell House. CHURCHILL *is painting. He sits before the full gear: easel, paintbox on a folding table, large palette, all under a huge umbrella.*

MACMILLAN, *in a mackintosh, with an umbrella, approaches.*

For a while they both stare at the canvas.

CHURCHILL. Can't do cows.

MACMILLAN. They're very good.

A beat.

Somewhat...

CHURCHILL. Somewhat what?

MACMILLAN. Legless.

CHURCHILL. They're sitting down!

MACMILLAN. Ah. Yes, I see.

CHURCHILL. Obviously they are sitting down!

MACMILLAN. The cows in the field are standing up.

CHURCHILL. But in my picture they are not!

MACMILLAN. Artistic licence.

CHURCHILL. What?

They look at each other.

A beat.

MACMILLAN. Winston, the Canal...

Nothing.

The Suez Canal.

Nothing.

The crisis!

CHURCHILL *is sunk in his thoughts, not moving.*

A beat.

Then MACMILLAN *can wait no longer...*

Win...

CHURCHILL *(interrupting)*. Colonel Nasser. Did I ever meet him?

MACMILLAN. I don't think so.

CHURCHILL. A Mussolini.

MACMILLAN. Anthony thinks more an Arab Hitler.

CHURCHILL. No. More tinpot. A Mussolini. That fat king.

MACMILLAN. What fat king?

CHURCHILL. The one Nasser kicked out. Farouk. Met him, in the war. Fingers like barrage balloons, with rings. Did we put him in power?

MACMILLAN. Of course. Don't you...

CHURCHILL *(interrupting)*. Had a splendid palace at Luxor, did things with boys in it. Had a private casino too. If I'd been a young Egyptian Army colonel in 1952, think I'd have kicked the bastard out...

MACMILLAN. Winston, there is a plan to get the Canal back.

CHURCHILL. Well, after three months of dithering with the United Nations I should damn well hope there is!

MACMILLAN. It's... a bold plan.

CHURCHILL. Involving Israel and France.

MACMILLAN. You know?

CHURCHILL. Israel attacks Egypt. England and France intervene to separate the Israeli and the Egyptian forces. To keep the Canal open and undamaged. On behalf of the international community, blah blah. In effect, we invade Egypt and get rid of Nasser.

MACMILLAN. Only four of us in the Cabinet know that, including Anthony. How did you find out?

CHURCHILL. Too gaga to remember.

He grins.

MACMILLAN. So what do you think?

CHURCHILL. Got a nip?

MACMILLAN (*taking out a flask*). Yes, actually...

CHURCHILL *takes the flask.*

CHURCHILL. Clemmie won't let me take alcohol out when I'm painting. I think she fears I'll produce some disastrous, late-abstract period. Or that it'll kill me. At last.

CHURCHILL *drinks. Then...*

The night Nasser took over the Canal.

MACMILLAN. Yes...

CHURCHILL. Made that huge speech in Alexandria, over the radio, all over the Middle East, crowd going wild...

MACMILLAN. Yes...

CHURCHILL. Kept on saying the name of the man who built the Canal. Man who built the bloody thing, help me here...

MACMILLAN. Ferdinand de Lesseps.

CHURCHILL. 'Ferdinand de Lesseps.' Said it fourteen times, no one could understand why. Turned out to be the signal for the Egyptian Army to take the Canal.

MACMILLAN. So what is your...

CHURCHILL (*interrupting*). What happened two hours later?

MACMILLAN. Anthony called a crisis meeting in Downing Street.

CHURCHILL. That meeting was his great mistake.

MACMILLAN. I think I follow.

CHURCHILL. You damn well should, you were there! First meeting after a crisis breaks, that's when success is grasped. Or not. At that crucial, deadly moment, there were ships and marines at Malta. They could have been at the Canal in four days. But he dithered.

MACMILLAN. So if you'd still been in Number Ten...

CHURCHILL. Don't let's play 'ifs'.

MACMILLAN. No.

A beat.

CHURCHILL. Oh, bugger it. 'If' the Labour Party hadn't won the '45 Election. 'If' I had stood down as Party Leader and Anthony had beaten Labour in 1951. 'If' I hadn't waited until '55 to resign as Prime Minister. 'If' it hadn't been Anthony who took over from me, but you.

A beat.

How worried about him are you?

MACMILLAN. He's taking a lot of pills.

CHURCHILL. Pills? When I was PM, I smoked seven cigars a day, drank three bottles of Pol Roger and much brandy, what are pills?

MACMILLAN. Anthony is a wonderful political animal, a Derby winner we've put our money on for years. The trouble is he was trained for the 1938 Derby. And only got out of the traps in 1955.

CHURCHILL. Very bitchy of you, Harold.

MACMILLAN. I know.

CHURCHILL. There a lot of bitching going on in Cabinet?

MACMILLAN. The atmosphere is highly unpleasant.

CHURCHILL. Moved you from the Foreign Office, didn't he?

Wanted a doormat. Selwyn Lloyd. Always wondered if Selwyn's simple in the head.

MACMILLAN. He's excellent.

CHURCHILL. Hunh. Those things.

MACMILLAN. Things...

CHURCHILL. Things you've brought in...

MACMILLAN. Do you mean Premium Bonds?

CHURCHILL. Those things. Brilliant. The British love a flutter. Combine saving with gambling, a winner. Anthony must be green.

MACMILLAN. I want to encourage savers.

CHURCHILL. You want to make Anthony sick!

MACMILLAN. I don't know. Why do we fight so?

CHURCHILL. Fear.

A beat.

We can't lose the Canal. Lose the Canal, we lose the Empire.

MACMILLAN. Yes.

CHURCHILL. Our place in the eyes of the world.

MACMILLAN. Particularly the eyes of the Americans.

CHURCHILL. Push him, Harold. Use the jockey's whip on this pill popping, broken down Derby favourite of ours. The British flag over Suez Town. Nasser dead. Black swans.

MACMILLAN. What?

CHURCHILL. I can turn these cows into swans. Have you seen our black swans here at Chartwell?

MACMILLAN. Many times...

CHURCHILL. Black swans, flying in the foreground.

CHURCHILL, *hunched over his easel, still painting, exits.*

The Cabinet Table enters. EDEN *is sitting in the Prime Minister's chair.*

YOUNG MAC (*aside*). The 25th of October, 1956. 10 Downing Street. Doggy be good, doggy be good.

The intercom buzzes. EDEN *flicks a switch. Throughout the scene he bullies the intercom.*

EDEN. What?

INTERCOM VOICE. Prime Minister, the Foreign Secretary is here.

EDEN. Then send him in at once!

MACMILLAN. Anthony, is there a record?

EDEN. Record?

MACMILLAN. A log.

EDEN. Yes, I see what you mean.

He clicks the switch on the intercom.

Did you log the call from RAF Northolt, confirming the Foreign Secretary's plane had landed?

INTERCOM VOICE. Yes…

EDEN. Destroy it. There is to be no record of the Foreign Secretary's flight to Paris. No log, no record.

INTERCOM VOICE. Of course, Prime…

EDEN *clicks the intercom off.*

Enter SELWYN LLOYD.

LLOYD. Good evening, Prime Minister. Harold.

EDEN. Selwyn, thank God. Have you eaten?

LLOYD. Not a thing since lunch.

EDEN *clicks the intercom.*

EDEN. Mrs Mason, tell the butler to bring some kind of cold collation. There was that guinea fowl?

INTERCOM VOICE. Certainly, Prime Minister.

EDEN *clicks the intercom off.*

MACMILLAN. You look like you could do with a drink.

LLOYD. I must admit I'm dying for a Scotch.

They look at EDEN.

EDEN. You know my rule, no alcohol in the Cabinet Room.
After those terrible last days with Winston.

LLOYD. Weren't they hell on earth…

EDEN. But tonight, I think, to celebrate our secret mission?

LLOYD. Yes. Secret mission. That's what I've been on.

MACMILLAN. Was it thrilling?

LLOYD. What?

MACMILLAN. Well, we are international conspirators.

LLOYD. Oh God, we are.

EDEN *clicks the intercom.*

INTERCOM VOICE. Prime Minister?

EDEN. Have the butler bring in a MacLennan with the food.
Three glasses.

Clicks the intercom off before a reply.

A beat.

How was the Israeli Prime Minister?

LLOYD. A pain in the backside. Kept on quoting Plato.

MACMILLAN. Ben-Gurion's a very cultured man.

LLOYD. That may be, but I think the long flight from Tel Aviv
had worn him out.

MACMILLAN. Did he have any military staff with him?

LLOYD. General Moshe Dayan.

EDEN. Dayan! Then the Israelis are serious.

LLOYD. Oh, they are serious all right. They want us to bomb Cairo.

A beat.

EDEN. Well, good. MI6 are certain the Egyptians haven't got wind of anything. Nasser still thinks we're all meeting in Geneva next week for a peace conference.

LLOYD *is uneasy.*

MACMILLAN. Selwyn, I hope you don't mind me saying so, but you have that look.

LLOYD. What look?

MACMILLAN. That 'don't blame me' look. What is the matter?

LLOYD. Dayan doesn't like what we are doing. He says it's collusion.

MACMILLAN. Well, that's the point of Anthony's plan, isn't it? The world must see Israel attack Egypt. Then see Britain and France intervene to separate them. And we bomb Port Said, land paratroops, and take the Canal back. As peacemakers.

LLOYD. But do you really think 'the world' will believe we are peacemakers?

MACMILLAN. The Labour Party won't, but that's neither here nor there.

LLOYD. And the Americans? I mean, when we say 'the world', we do mean America, don't we?

The intercom light flashes. EDEN *flicks the switch.*

EDEN. What in hell's name is it now?

INTERCOM VOICE. The food, Prime Minister…

EDEN. Well, send it in!

Enter a BUTLER, *carrying a plate of food covered with a silver lid, a bottle of whisky, a soda siphon and three glasses. He wears white gloves.*

Ah, Milburn.

The BUTLER *puts the tray on the table. He lifts the bottle of whisky.* MACMILLAN *watches him closely.*

No, we'll help ourselves.

BUTLER (*a Lancashire accent*). Will there be anything else, Prime Minister?

EDEN. No, thank you so much.

BUTLER. Thank you, gentlemen.

MACMILLAN. You're new at Number Ten.

BUTLER. Yes, sir.

MACMILLAN. That pin in your lapel. 8th Army Corps? You fought in North Africa?

BUTLER. Garrison at Tobruk, sir.

MACMILLAN. Well, good show.

BUTLER. Thank you, sir.

The BUTLER *goes.*

MACMILLAN. Where did you find him?

EDEN. Recuperating at Headley Court. Terrible burns, you should see his hands without the gloves.

LLOYD. He carries a tray.

EDEN. What?

LLOYD. Even with his hands he still buttles.

EDEN. Well, obviously.

EDEN *and* MACMILLAN *are momentarily at a loss.*

LLOYD. Forgive me, I... am tired beyond damnation.

MACMILLAN *pours a drink for* LLOYD *and hands it to him as* EDEN *speaks.*

EDEN. Selwyn, everything is ready. The French fleet sailed from Algiers five days ago, today I had the report their paratroops have airlifted to Cyprus. Our Canberra bombers there have ordinance and fuel for two hundred sorties. Our troop ships are near to their station off the Egyptian coast. All will be well, all manner of things... if you can tell me good news.

LLOYD. The Israelis agreed to the plan.

MACMILLAN *smiles,* EDEN *raises his hands in triumph.*

So now it's up to you. Whether we go ahead or not.

EDEN. Well, of course we go ahead!

MACMILLAN. Selwyn, you do think we are right to attack? I mean, in the past you've argued Nasser is the devil incarnate!

LLOYD. It's that, after the invasion, I mean... we'll find the Egyptian economy wrecked, railways, roads, communications largely destroyed, there will be disease... I think we do need some kind of plan. I mean, victory's all very well, but what do we do then?

MACMILLAN. Is this you talking, or the Chief of the Armed Services?

LLOYD. General Keightley did bend my ear.

EDEN. Keightley's a damn old woman.

LLOYD. He does have a point. The occupation force we will need will be huge. National Service will have to carry on, which could prove to be very unpopular...

EDEN. Will you shut up!

A beat.

MACMILLAN. We must hold on to one simple thing. This is a direct challenge by a third-world country to Britain's power. We cannot let it pass. The British Empire's blood flows through the Suez Canal.

EDEN. No, we can't have it in the hands of some Arab...

EDEN *makes an irritable gesture.*

LLOYD. Mussolini?

EDEN. Hitler.

LLOYD. I will support whatever decision you make, Prime Minister.

A beat.

I don't think I'll eat this. I must catch up on some sleep.

EDEN. Of course. You're welcome to use the flat upstairs…

LLOYD. I think I'll go home for a few hours.

EDEN. Yes, why don't you.

LLOYD. Telephone me if there's… anything.

EDEN. Yes.

LLOYD *exits*.

Selwyn's like a snappy little dog worrying at a bone!

MACMILLAN. He's fine.

EDEN. He is loyal, isn't he?

MACMILLAN. More… faithful. Selwyn's one of those men who cannot conceive of having any master other than the one he has. It's a virtue. Alcohol?

EDEN. Oh dear God, yes please.

MACMILLAN *pours drinks for them.* EDEN *downs his and reaches for the bottle.* MACMILLAN *observes but turns away.*

You saw Winston.

MACMILLAN. Yes, actually.

EDEN. '… Actually.'

MACMILLAN. As a matter of interest, how did you know?

EDEN. Drivers report all journeys ministers make to the Cabinet Office.

MACMILLAN. Since when?

EDEN. Since me.

MACMILLAN. Well. Then it's fortunate I haven't visited any bordellos.

EDEN. Unlike some.

And EDEN *drinks deeply.*

How is the Old Man?

MACMILLAN. There is... slippage.

EDEN. He thinks I'm dithering.

MACMILLAN. He understands your need to attack Egypt with some justification in international law.

EDEN. Admit it, Harold.

MACMILLAN. Admit what?

EDEN. Admit you're bitter I put Selwyn in the Foreign Office, not you.

MACMILLAN. Anthony, I'm perfectly happy next door. Fascinating thing, the economy. Almost mystical. Being Chancellor of the Exchequer is rather like being a priest in Ancient Rome, staring at the entrails of a slaughtered goat. You are sure that if you read the mess in front of you right, you will know the future.

EDEN. And what future did you see, staring at entrails with Winston?

YOUNG MAC. Black swans.

MACMILLAN. Success. The Empire secure. International law upheld. And Nasser dead.

EDEN *is staring at him.*

EDEN. I bought ten of your Premium Bonds.

MACMILLAN. Any luck?

EDEN. Not a penny.

The Cabinet Table, EDEN *sitting at it, veers away.*

DANCERS *enter. They jive to Elvis Presley's 'Hound Dog'.*

Then DOROTHY *and* BOOTHBY *enter, making their way through the* DANCERS, *very merry. They embrace passionately, pulling at each other's clothes. They go down upon the floor as...*

MACMILLAN *makes his way through the* DANCERS *and stands over* DOROTHY *and* BOOTHBY.

The DANCERS *scatter.*

DOROTHY *and* BOOTHBY *look at* MACMILLAN. *Then they stand and are putting their clothes to rights.*

MACMILLAN. Must you do this in the Ritz?

DOROTHY. You didn't let us know you were coming.

MACMILLAN. One's movements are unpredictable in a crisis.

DOROTHY. Yes, aren't they?

BOOTHBY. Harold, I...

DOROTHY (*interrupting*). Well, I expect you and Bob...

MACMILLAN. It's you I want to see, actually.

A beat.

BOOTHBY (*to* MACMILLAN). I'll be at Whites until midnight if you need me.

MACMILLAN. Thank you.

BOOTHBY *turns to go but hesitates.*

BOOTHBY. How serious is the thing in Hungary?

MACMILLAN. Russian tanks have reached Budapest.

BOOTHBY. The worst time, with the Canal...

MACMILLAN. Absolutely.

BOOTHBY. I heard a rumour General Dayan's massing tanks on the Egyptian border. Are the Israelis going to get involved?

MACMILLAN. Club-room tittle-tattle. And rather dangerous nonsense.

A beat.

BOOTHBY. Well, if you, or Selwyn, or Anthony do need me...

MACMILLAN. Whites, yes. Bob, do you use Government cars?

BOOTHBY. I'm just a lowly chairman of a Commons committee...

MACMILLAN. Committee chairmen have been known to wangle cars from the pool.

BOOTHBY. Well...

MACMILLAN. It's just that if you do, your driver will have to report where you've been.

BOOTHBY. I see.

A beat.

And BOOTHBY *exits.*

DOROTHY. Bob is very discreet, you know.

MACMILLAN. So I observe.

Her blouse is still unbuttoned. She turns away, fixes it then turns back to MACMILLAN.

DOROTHY. What can I help you with, Harold?

MACMILLAN. I believe you had tea at Number Ten with Clarissa, two days ago?

DOROTHY. What of it?

MACMILLAN. This is really rather difficult.

DOROTHY. Just pretend it isn't.

MACMILLAN. No, I mean, what I want to ask is difficult. Of you and me, I really am past caring.

DOROTHY. No you're not.

A beat.

MACMILLAN. When you saw her, did Clarissa say anything about Anthony's health?

DOROTHY. Why do you all spy on each other?

MACMILLAN. Because we are terrified things will fall apart, that is why. Only when you're at the heart of Government do you realise how close chaos is.

A beat.

DOROTHY. Anthony drinks. And takes amphetamines. He hides them. She finds herself rummaging in his clothes at night, looking for bottles of tablets.

MACMILLAN. Dear God.

DOROTHY. He doesn't sleep. In the middle of the night he goes into rages against anyone: a window cleaner who came that day, the Israeli Prime Minister, the entire American nation, the Cabinet, you. He really rages against you.

MACMILLAN. Why?

DOROTHY. He thinks you are plotting with Winston.

MACMILLAN. That's absurd.

DOROTHY. Is it?

MACMILLAN. Yes!

DOROTHY. He weeps in her arms, Harold. The wartime darling of the British people, Winston's natural successor, the man who was going to bring a new age of hope and glamour into politics, weeps in his wife's arms like a baby. One of you will have to take over.

MACMILLAN. That is ridiculous, unthinkable, we are in the middle of an international crisis.

DOROTHY. If Anthony breaks down completely, it will have to be Rab or Ian or you. And it has to be you, Harold. At last live up to what you should be.

MACMILLAN. I didn't realise the role of an adulterous wife was to sound like one's dead mother.

A beat.

That's unworthy of me.

DOROTHY. Yes.

MACMILLAN. Anthony will come through. For all his faults, he has one thing: bravery, tested bravery. This is a man who got the Military Cross at Ypres.

DOROTHY. So important to you men, isn't it, who was riddled with bullets, who was not.

MACMILLAN. Mock if you must. But I think I can only trust people who know what war is.

DOROTHY. I'm not mocking you. I'm not. But Harold, if you're so confident in your hero, why are you asking secretly about his health?

A beat.

MACMILLAN. I must go back to Number Ten.

He turns away.

DOROTHY *exits.*

The Cabinet Table, EDEN *still seated, veers into sight.*

Enter to one side EISENHOWER – *in a suit* – *with three* AIDES. *They are all listening to telephone extensions – the technology of the time. They move around* EISENHOWER.

EDEN, MACMILLAN *and* LLOYD *are listening with similar devices, plugged into the intercom box.*

YOUNG MAC *is still beneath the table.*

YOUNG MAC *(aside).* October the 29th. Doggy being good. Chasing Israeli tanks in the sand, woof woof! Happy dog.

INTERCOM VOICE. President Eisenhower is on the Washington hotline now, Prime Minister.

EISENHOWER. Anthony, how are you?

EDEN. Deeply concerned, Mr President, as you can imagine.

An AIDE *moves across to* EISENHOWER *and hands him a card. He glances at it and hands it back.*

EISENHOWER. I have to ask you, er, this, Anthony. Did you have any indication the Israelis were going to attack Egypt?

EDEN. None whatsoever.

LLOYD *looks at* MACMILLAN, *who grins.*

EISENHOWER*'s* AIDES *look at each other, concerned. One of them scribbles a word quickly on a card and hands it to* EISENHOWER, *who glances at it and hands it back.*

EISENHOWER. Well, I have to be frank here. We have been, er, picking up a heck of a lot of traffic between Paris and Tel Aviv. It could look like the French knew the Israelis were going to attack.

LLOYD (*low*). Oh my God.

EISENHOWER. We're all meant to be allies, but we're in a sad state of confusion here. This action could destabilise the whole of the Arab world.

MACMILLAN (*low, to* EDEN). You have to put it to him.

EDEN *hesitates.*

Now, Anthony!

As EDEN *speaks, a fourth* AIDE *to* EISENHOWER *enters with a telex message. He hands it to* EISENHOWER *who stares at it. Then he hands it to the other* AIDES *who pass it quickly amongst themselves.*

EDEN. Mr President, what Great Britain cannot afford is to see the Canal closed, or to lose the shipping that daily passes through it. We feel that decisive action should be taken at once, to stop the hostilities.

A beat.

Mr President?

EISENHOWER. Anthony, we have a report that Israeli troops are being parachuted in on the Suez zone.

An AIDE *points at the telex in front of him.*

No, that's on Suez Town.

LLOYD. How could he know that so quickly?

MACMILLAN. The CIA must be listening in on the Israeli High Command.

EISENHOWER. In... you know from our victory against Hitler's Germany, what I believe in is the whole orchestra, playing together. We have Russian tanks in Hungary, we have Israeli tanks in Egypt. At a moment like this we must play together.

EDEN (*staring at* MACMILLAN). Dwight, I am absolutely at one with what you say.

EISENHOWER. Well, I'm sure we'll speak in a few hours' time.

EISENHOWER *goes into a huddle with his* AIDES.

EDEN. He doesn't know our ships are ready to attack. Or that our bombers are on Cyprus.

MACMILLAN. No. The U2 spy planes can't be over the Mediterranean.

LLOYD. Yet.

MACMILLAN. Forty-eight hours and our troops will be in. We must hold our nerve.

EISENHOWER *exits fast, his* AIDES *around him in a huddle*.

LLOYD *exits*.

The BUTLER *enters with a large silver tray. It is full of dirty plates, crumpled napkins, an empty bottle of whisky. He sets the mess on the table*.

EDEN *and* MACMILLAN *finish eating*.

EDEN. I met Nasser, you know.

MACMILLAN. Really? When?

EDEN. Two years ago in Cairo. There was a dinner at the British Embassy.

MACMILLAN. What was your impression?

EDEN. I liked him. There was something... manly, something dynamic about him. He had charm.

MACMILLAN. That's what they always said about...

EDEN. Hitler, yes. The Egyptians didn't dress for dinner.
Nasser wore uniform, the others were in rather shabby
lounge suits. Unnecessarily aggressive, I thought.

MACMILLAN. I can imagine.

EDEN. Hitler dreamt of wild horses.

MACMILLAN. How do you know that?

A beat.

They look at each other.

EDEN. I just know. Nasser dreams of a necklace of pearls.

MACMILLAN. I...

EDEN. Arab unity. He'll begin by uniting Egypt with Syria,
then Jordan. And end ruling from Morocco in the west to
Iraq in the east. A modern Islamic Empire. It could be more
powerful than Europe, with three-quarters of the world's oil.
He sees it. At night. A necklace of nations, on a beautiful
woman, the lights of the shutters in his house across her skin,
as he fondles her throat...

He stares at nothing.

MACMILLAN. Anthony...

LLOYD *enters at speed, a telex in his hand.*

LLOYD. The Americans have tabled a resolution at the Security
Council. It demands that Israel stops fighting immediately
and withdraws from Egypt.

EDEN. But that will wreck... Why didn't the Americans tell us
they were going to do this?

MACMILLAN. We'll veto the American resolution.

LLOYD. That is a drastic and dangerous course.

MACMILLAN. Telling the Americans to stuff it? Be wildly
popular.

They look at EDEN, who is staring straight ahead.

LLOYD. Anthony?

MACMILLAN. We have no choice.

LLOYD. I want the Prime Minister's opinion, Harold! Not yours!

A beat.

EDEN. No. No choice.

LLOYD. Anthony, I'm going to have to give instructions to our ambassador in the Security Council. I'm damned if I know what to tell him to say. This morning we sent the ultimatum to Israel and Egypt demanding that the fighting stop. We can't turn round on the same day and veto a United Nations resolution that asks for the same thing!

EDEN. Yes, but Israel may feel they cannot disobey a UN resolution. If they stop fighting, there'll be no reason for us going in. No! No! No more being blown this way and that! This is the time of hazard. We must keep our eyes on the great prize.

MACMILLAN. Knocking Nasser for six.

Enter the British invasion of Egypt at the back of the stage.

Small-arms fire.

Three SOLDIERS *of a Parachute Brigade back onto the stage, pulling down parachutes and bundling them up.*

There is the constant crack of small-arms fire.

The 1ST SOLDIER *slings a radio set – large, camouflaged, cumbersome – from his back and hurriedly tries to make it work.*

2ND SOLDIER. Enemy fire! Enemy fire!

3RD SOLDIER. Fucking small arms! That fucking wall, three hundred yards!

1ST SOLDIER. Blue Sector to Red Bravo. Blue Sector to Red Bravo. Fuck!

He bangs the radio as the 2ND SOLDIER *is hit, doubling over.*

2ND SOLDIER. I'm hit, in my hand, my fucking hand…

He screams.

1ST SOLDIER. Blue Sector to Red Bravo.

… and there is a loud explosion.

3RD SOLDIER. Fucking mortar, they've got a fucking
mortar…

1ST SOLDIER. Cover, that building two hundred yards…

3RD SOLDIER. What's that fucking smell?

The 2ND SOLDIER, *weeping, slings the radio over his
shoulder, and the* 1ST SOLDIER *helps him. They carry their
parachutes.*

Another mortar round goes off.

The SOLDIERS *exit.*

While this happens, the BUTLER *clears the Cabinet Table
and sets a map upon it. There is still a bottle of whisky and
three glasses.*

MACMILLAN *and* EDEN *are looking at the map.* EDEN
raises a glass. His hand begins to shake uncontrollably.
MACMILLAN *glances at the intercom – should he call for
help? – but* EDEN *controls his breathing.*

EDEN. Do you fish?

MACMILLAN. Anthony?

EDEN. Fish!

MACMILLAN. Not much. Shoot, of course, Scotland, every
New Year's.

EDEN. We've never done that together. What's your usual bag?

MACMILLAN. A hundred and fifty pheasants or so. Not
woodcock, I've never seen the point.

EDEN. When this is over, I'll take you fly-fishing. The River
Avon.

MACMILLAN. I would enjoy that.

EDEN. Do something peaceful, English.

MACMILLAN. Kill birds and fish.

EDEN. Absolutely.

They laugh, for a moment just friends.

LLOYD *enters quickly with a telegram.*

Ah. Our professional bringer of bad news.

LLOYD. No, good news, Prime Minister! A telegram.

He holds it up – an echo of CHAMBERLAIN*'s iconic gesture.*

YOUNG MAC. Seen a Government minister hold up a bit of paper before, when was that, when was that?

MACMILLAN *snatches the telegram from* LLOYD*'s hand and reads.*

MACMILLAN. It's a flash signal from General Keightley.

He reads it and looks up.

Anthony, congratulations.

LLOYD. A knock-out, you've knocked Nasser out...

EDEN. Give me that! Give it to me!

EDEN *snatches the telegram and reads it. For a moment he is frozen, then very active.*

I'll go straight to the House and make a statement. Stuff this down the Labour Party's throat!

LLOYD. Oh, that will feel so good...

EDEN. Then I want all my Service Chiefs here at Number Ten. We'll have something of a party. Harold, Selwyn, I thank you from the bottom of my heart. I never wanted to be a wartime Prime Minister. It's peace I want.

MACMILLAN. We know that.

EDEN. But this is a great moment! Victory is in our grasp!

LLOYD. And the Labour Party won't know what's hit them! I hope it's Aneurin Bevan who speaks. Oh, I so want to see Bevan debagged, flour and treacle all over his balls.

EDEN. Oh, we'll debag the windbag.

All three of them laugh.

EDEN *and* LLOYD *exit.* MACMILLAN *hesitates and looks back at* YOUNG MAC, *crouched under the table.*

YOUNG MAC. You know it's coming. Any moment now.

MACMILLAN. No, we will take the Canal.

YOUNG MAC. You saw it in North Africa. Clear day. No wind. The sandstorm just a smudge, miles away. Then suddenly... blindness.

MACMILLAN. No! All is well.

MACMILLAN *exits. The Cabinet Table slides away.*

11 Downing Street.

MACMILLAN *enters. He carries a telephone, trailing a long wire.*

YOUNG MAC *enters and sulks at the back.*

A beat.

CROOKSHANK *enters.*

CROOKSHANK. Harold.

MACMILLAN. Harry, thank you for coming over.

CROOKSHANK. The news from the Canal is wonderful.

MACMILLAN. Isn't it?

CROOKSHANK. Did Keightley expect it to be so easy?

MACMILLAN. We have far superior forces.

CROOKSHANK. I thought you'd be next door. Anthony's got all the Chiefs there. Lashings of Pol Roger, I hear, just like the old days with Winston. Shall we pop round...

MACMILLAN. Harry, I have to warn you.

CROOKSHANK. Warn?

MACMILLAN. There may be a difficult time ahead for our party in the House, and in the country. As you're Chief Whip I think you had better be prepared.

CROOKSHANK. Prepared for what?

MACMILLAN. The worst.

A beat.

CROOKSHANK. Harold…

MACMILLAN. No, this is just…

CROOKSHANK. What are you talking about…?

MACMILLAN. Just to flag up –

CROOKSHANK. 'Flag up…'?

MACMILLAN. – a possible situation.

A beat.

CROOKSHANK. Are you talking about… some kind of defeat?

MACMILLAN. I just want to know whether, if we get into a really bloody situation, you'll be loyal to me.

CROOKSHANK. To you? I'm Government Chief Whip! I'm loyal to the Prime Minister.

MACMILLAN. Yes, of course. We all are.

CROOKSHANK. While… he is Prime Minister.

MACMILLAN. Absolutely.

CROOKSHANK. Dear God, Harold, what's happened?

MACMILLAN. The question is, what is about to happen? You are my most trusted old comrade in the House. Can I rely on you?

A beat.

CROOKSHANK. Yes.

MACMILLAN. I have to take a telephone call now.

CROOKSHANK. I'll be at my office in the House until I hear from you.

MACMILLAN. Good.

CROOKSHANK *exits*.

MACMILLAN *looks at his watch*.

The clock chimes the half hour. It finishes and at once the telephone rings.

YOUNG MAC. Goodbye, British Empire.

MACMILLAN *lifts the telephone*.

At the back of the stage, EISENHOWER *enters with a telephone, his* AIDES *with listening devices.*

EISENHOWER. Harold, are you on the line?

MACMILLAN. Yes, Mr President.

The passing back and forth of cards between EISEN-HOWER *and his* AIDES *begins, as earlier in the scene.*

EISENHOWER. Good to speak to you, as ever.

MACMILLAN. Good to hear you too, Dwight.

EISENHOWER. I wish this was an easier call to make. I want this to be strictly between ourselves. I mean, I'm going behind your Prime Minister's back here, if you're uncomfortable with that, you had better say.

A beat.

MACMILLAN. Please go on.

EISENHOWER. We've done our best here. But I think the British Government is making one of the biggest errors of our time. Outside of us losing China.

MACMILLAN. Dwight, Britain has special interests.

EISENHOWER. If you occupy Egypt, the Soviets could intervene and we'll have a global crisis.

MACMILLAN. Our crisis is that we're in danger of losing the route for our oil.

EISENHOWER. You've got to take the broader view.

MACMILLAN. We can't afford to. Oil is our lifeblood.

EISENHOWER. Hell, Harold, Nasser ran the Canal perfectly well for three months before you attacked. Your ships weren't threatened.

MACMILLAN. But with the Canal in Egypt's hands they always can be. Look what Nasser's done in the last four days: sunk forty ships, blocking the entire waterway.

EISENHOWER. Well, naturally he's blocked the Canal, you've invaded his country!

MACMILLAN. It's a peacekeeping operation...

EISENHOWER. Please, Harold, don't demean your intelligence and mine.

A beat. The AIDES *are still.*

MACMILLAN. Dwight, America has her spheres of influence, we have ours. And the Middle East is very much a British sphere of influence. It's the Imperial burden, but Britain has borne it proudly.

EISENHOWER. Jesus fucking Christ, Harold... 'spheres of influence'? Actually, America's only got one now, since the War. Just one 'sphere of influence'. The whole damn planet.

Two AIDES *are holding out cards in front of the angry* EISENHOWER. *He waves them all away. They hesitate, he waves them away again.*

The AIDES *exit.*

MACMILLAN. Dwight?

EISENHOWER. Harold, personally you've put up a good fight here. But I have to tell you that if the British forces do not stop fighting in the next twenty-four hours, I will instruct the Federal Reserve Bank of America to start selling British sterling. We will then go on selling until there is a ceasefire.

How long do you think it will be until your British pound is totally worthless?

MACMILLAN. Oh… three days?

EISENHOWER. The Fed say two.

MACMILLAN. That would be an act of economic warfare against an ally.

EISENHOWER. More a kick up the butt of an old friend.

MACMILLAN. I don't believe you'll do this.

EISENHOWER. Try me.

Simultaneously they break the link. They each look at their telephones for a moment, in shock. Then EISENHOWER *exits.*

YOUNG MAC *is at the back.*

MACMILLAN *turns.*

The Cabinet Table enters, EDEN *seated.* MACMILLAN *stands by the table.*

EDEN *suddenly stands.*

EDEN. Stop?

A beat.

Stop?

A beat.

But our troops haven't even got out of Port Said! Stop!?

MACMILLAN. We have to. The pound is selling in all the markets. We can't defend it. Our reserves will be gone in under forty-eight hours, the pound will be worthless.

EDEN. We'll ask the American Federal Reserve to intervene…

MACMILLAN. Anthony, it's the Reserve who began the selling and they're still doing it.

EDEN. Well, Harold, borrow from the International Monetary Fund!

MACMILLAN. I've tried, but the Americans are blocking my efforts.

EDEN. I'll telephone Eisenhower at once.

MACMILLAN. I think you'll find he won't speak to you.

EDEN. Why are they doing this to us?

MACMILLAN. To force us to call a ceasefire.

EDEN. No. No. We're equal partners.

MACMILLAN. As Chancellor of the Exchequer, I have to tell you, if we do not call a ceasefire, Britain will be bankrupt.

A beat.

EDEN. But you were for the invasion! You were the most gung-ho of all of us!

MACMILLAN. We must face reality.

EDEN. What reality is that? Defeat? Humiliation? The end of the Empire's role in the world? What?

MACMILLAN. We must stop. We have no choice. I think a majority of the party in the House will agree.

EDEN. Oh, do you?

MACMILLAN. I've taken soundings.

EDEN. Oh, have you?

MACMILLAN. And the Cabinet will agree to a ceasefire.

EDEN. What, more 'soundings'?

He realises.

Your pal, your old army pal, Harry Crookshank! You've turned the Chief Whip against me...

MACMILLAN. We have to address the situation...

EDEN. Judas.

MACMILLAN. I'm sorry?

EDEN. Judas!

MACMILLAN. Anthony, at this moment that is not a helpful remark.

EDEN. Really? Have I made an unhelpful remark? Like, 'Stop that sand-nigger Nasser and save the British Empire', oh dear. Sorry, I'm dreadfully sorry, give me a moment, please.

A beat.

MACMILLAN. Anthony, we must send a flash signal to General Keightley...

EDEN. You've been waiting for me to fail. All along.

MACMILLAN. On the contrary, I desperately wanted you to succeed.

EDEN. Gung-ho, all along. Knowing that when I went down, your time would come!

MACMILLAN. This is a catastrophe that we all made, Anthony. We must pick up and save what we can.

EDEN. But not save me, I think. I won't go quietly. It will have to be a 'knives on the steps of the Capitol' job! You up to that?

MACMILLAN. Judas and Brutus, all in one?

EDEN. Are you up to it!?

MACMILLAN. Yes.

A beat.

If it is necessary. Yes.

EDEN. Just like when we did for poor Neville.

EDEN *deflates. A beat.*

Illness, I think, don't you?

MACMILLAN. I'd have thought so.

EDEN. The choice is wide, God knows there's enough wrong with me. But not now, not at once...

MACMILLAN. No, of course not.

EDEN. Give me a month or two. See the troops home.

MACMILLAN. Yes.

EDEN. I don't think I can do the Americans. The patching up.
I'll leave that to you.

MACMILLAN. I don't for a moment assume...

EDEN. Oh, it'll be yours. The prize. The great prize. The crown
of thorns.

He flicks the intercom.

I want to send a flash signal to General Keightley. Thank
you, Harold. I don't need you here.

MACMILLAN. No. Thank you, Prime Minister.

MACMILLAN *turns away.*

Alone, EDEN *puts his hand to his face and begins to weep.*

EDEN *still seated as the Cabinet Table veers away.* EDEN
exits.

MACMILLAN *is alone on the stage.*

End of Act Three.

ACT FOUR

Bodies Out of Control (1957-1963)

For a moment MACMILLAN *is alone. A glass of champagne is in his hand.*

MACMILLAN (*aside*). A feeling of intolerable sweetness.

A beat.

On the way back from the Palace, in the car, Her Majesty having asked me to form a Government as Prime Minister, I'm afraid I thought first of my mother. Would this, at last, have made her loving? Or silenced her? Now she's dead I think she dominates me more than when she was alive.

Sips.

And as the car went under Admiralty Arch, into Trafalgar Square, my mood was worse. I felt: this can't be for me. The sense that I should have died in the war when I was young has never left me. For a moment I thought: order the car to turn around, go back to the Palace, make some kind of apology, I'm just a duffer from Eton, I shouldn't even be alive, I'm... What was it Dorothy said once? A klutz. 'I am a klutz, Your Majesty...'

A beat.

And then, as the car turned into Downing Street, and there were crowds cheering, all that melted away. And there was only... the sweetness of power.

An echo of the scene in Act One when CHURCHILL *came to power. A* CROWD, *supporters and the staff at 10 Downing Street, men and women, enter and come forward, all smiling. There is clapping. They are led by* DOROTHY, CROOK-SHANK, LLOYD *and* BOOTHBY, *who are all in evening dress. Two* WAITERS *distribute champagne.*

YOUNG MAC (*close to* MACMILLAN). Remember Winston, when he came to Number Ten. Pull a Winston.

MACMILLAN. Thank you all for the welcome. Many are saying my Government won't last more than six weeks. Be that as it may, I want... to set a more relaxed tone here at Number Ten. To that end, I want the staff to understand clearly that the drinking of non-vintage champagne will be severely reprimanded.

A moment's shock, then delighted laughter.

I have a Grand Design. First, we steady the country, heal the wound with America. Then we look to Europe. Britain at the centre of a united Europe was always Winston's vision – before he was so rudely interrupted by the Labour Party in 1945.

Smiles, laughter.

I will be announcing my Cabinet over the next few days, but I want to tell you that I have asked Mr Edward Heath to begin negotiations with our European friends, at once. Ted will fly to Paris this weekend to meet General de Gaulle, as I will at the earliest possibility. The Grand Design, my friends: Britain, back in her rightful place in the world, Britain restored!

He raises a glass.

They all raise glasses.

ALL. Britain restored!

They all drink and there are cheers and cries of 'Bravo'.

The CROWD *exit.*

DOROTHY, CROOKSHANK, LLOYD *and* BOOTHBY *stay.* DOROTHY *kisses* MACMILLAN *on the cheek.*

DOROTHY. Darling, so well done.

MACMILLAN. Thank you, my dear.

YOUNG MAC. Do her lover now.

MACMILLAN. Harry, I'll have the second half of the list by eleven o'clock.

CROOKSHANK. Thank you, Prime Minister.

YOUNG MAC. Do the lover!

MACMILLAN. Bob, could I have a word?

> DOROTHY *and* BOOTHBY *look at each other.* CROOK-SHANK, DOROTHY *and* LLOYD *exit.*

BOOTHBY. Prime Minister?

MACMILLAN. Ah.

YOUNG MAC. His eyes are shining. He hasn't had a drink this morning because he thinks you're going to make him Foreign Secretary! And you could. Even now. You'd just say: 'Bob, I'm sending you to the Foreign Office.'

MACMILLAN. Bob, I'm recommending to the Palace that you be given a peerage. I hope you will take it.

YOUNG MAC. Bom bom!

> YOUNG MAC *goes away.*

> *A beat.*

BOOTHBY. You're kicking me upstairs to the House of Lords?

MACMILLAN. I think you'll be effective there.

BOOTHBY. Effective doing what?

MACMILLAN. What you do best.

> *A beat.*

BOOTHBY. You're not offering me anything, are you?

MACMILLAN. I'm afraid not.

BOOTHBY. This is downright petty of you, Harold.

MACMILLAN. This isn't about you and Dorothy.

BOOTHBY. No?

MACMILLAN. No.

BOOTHBY. Then what the hell is it about?

MACMILLAN. Do you know a man called Ronald Kray?

A beat.

And his brother Reginald Kray?

BOOTHBY. I don't think I... What are they, Young Conservatives?

MACMILLAN. I've no idea of their politics. But to judge from their involvement in hijacking, armed robbery and arson, they are probably somewhat to the right of Hitler. You don't know them?

A beat.

In that case you've never been to any of the clubs they own. For example, a nightclub in Knightsbridge called 'Esmeralda's Barn'.

BOOTHBY. MI5 file, is it?

MACMILLAN. Yes.

BOOTHBY. I don't apologise for what I am.

MACMILLAN. Nor should any of us.

BOOTHBY. No.

A laugh at himself.

You know, a few minutes ago I was imagining you were about to offer me the Foreign Office.

MACMILLAN. I think you understand why that was always something of a remote possibility.

BOOTHBY. I'd have made a damn good Foreign Secretary.

MACMILLAN. No cordon sanitaire strong enough.

BOOTHBY. Sorry?

MACMILLAN. Nothing.

BOOTHBY. Can I ask who...?

MACMILLAN. Selwyn Lloyd.

BOOTHBY. Selwyn? Well. Since he'll be negotiating with the Americans, I suppose it's a good thing he doesn't sleep with homosexual gangsters in rooms above Knightsbridge clubs.

MACMILLAN. Yes, Americans can be horribly moralistic.

BOOTHBY. I will be loyal.

MACMILLAN. I know.

BOOTHBY. But I will still see Dorothy.

A beat.

MACMILLAN. That's as needs be.

BOOTHBY. Oh, we do need, Harold, she and I.

MACMILLAN. Be careful, Bob.

BOOTHBY. Is that a threat?

MACMILLAN. Absolutely.

A beat.

BOOTHBY. Thank you, Prime Minister.

YOUNG MAC. Sweetness.

BOOTHBY *exits.* CROOKSHANK *hurries on.*

CROOKSHANK. Prime Minister, President Eisenhower is on the hotline.

MACMILLAN. If I go to Washington it'll look like crawling to Daddy to say sorry for the Suez mess.

CROOKSHANK. We are sorry for the Suez mess.

MACMILLAN. Yes. But, as the weaker partner, we must meet on British soil. I think: Bermuda. Thank God we still run a few small islands.

MACMILLAN *and* CROOKSHANK *exit.*

Bermuda, 20th March, 1957. The Mid Ocean Club. Garden by the sea.

The British and American flags unfurl. Two MARINES, *one American, one British – in tropical pith helmet – march on and stand at attention.*

Evening effects: sunset, cicadas. A WAITER *with a tray; on it, a brandy bottle and a siphon.*

MACMILLAN *and* EISENHOWER *amble on in evening dress. They carry brandy glasses.* EISENHOWER *is smoking a cigar,* MACMILLAN *a cigarette.*

EISENHOWER. Excellent dinner, Harold. Yorkshire puddings and spotted dick in the tropics.

MACMILLAN. We call it 'comfort food'.

EISENHOWER. Comfort, we need.

A beat.

Beautiful sunset.

MACMILLAN. Yes.

EISENHOWER. They say it's the H-bomb tests in the Pacific, making sunsets round the world spectacular.

MACMILLAN. 'They'? You mean the anti-nuclear lobby?

EISENHOWER. No, our scientists say it. In secret, of course.

MACMILLAN. Yes.

EISENHOWER. A hell of a thing. Shall we go round the fences?

MACMILLAN. There are some holes.

EISENHOWER. Nothing we can't fix.

A beat.

The United Nations resolution, demanding that Israel withdraws completely from Egyptian soil. We want you to support it.

MACMILLAN. Ben-Gurion will see that as a betrayal.

EISENHOWER. Until those troops are out of the Sinai Desert, we can't begin to stabilise things in the Middle East.

MACMILLAN. It's a bitter pill.

EISENHOWER. All the pills are bitter, Harold.

MACMILLAN. Consider that one swallowed.

EISENHOWER. Good. Now we can put Suez behind us.

MACMILLAN. I agree.

EISENHOWER. You know, when you're in the top job, what others think is a scratch on the thigh, feels to you like a broken leg.

MACMILLAN. As I am beginning to learn.

They laugh, drink, smoke.

EISENHOWER. What, er, are your plans?

MACMILLAN. I will have to call a general election before too long. Then I can move. I will go to Africa. There's unfinished British business there. Then turn towards Europe.

EISENHOWER. Well, in any of your endeavours, Harold, you know you have a friend across the water. The Special Relationship is very real.

MACMILLAN. Shared values.

EISENHOWER. In a dangerous world.

MACMILLAN. Good. Then I can raise something with you? The question of nuclear secrets.

EISENHOWER. Right.

MACMILLAN. I'm asking you to share your atomic technology.

EISENHOWER. I'm afraid that there, Harold, we hit a wall.

MACMILLAN. But you've developed an H-bomb, so have we.

EISENHOWER. The problem is, Harold, we don't know whether you really have developed an H-bomb.

MACMILLAN. That is nonsense...

EISENHOWER. Our experts looked at the readings of your latest test explosion in the Pacific. I don't know how to put this... but we think you were faking it.

MACMILLAN. I assure you...

EISENHOWER. Come on, Harold, you've been talking up
your nuclear orgasms. Look, we'll give you sixty Thor
missiles. Operating on a two-key system, our finger, your
finger on the trigger.

MACMILLAN. But that means we are not an independent
nuclear power.

EISENHOWER. I know this is really about keeping Britain at
the top table. But... can I be blunt? You've got one reactor
at Windscale. Working way over the limit to produce
enough plutonium. Hell, the other month the damn thing
nearly blew up.

YOUNG MAC. Bully boy.

MACMILLAN. It was simple human error, the fire was put out.

EISENHOWER. To be even blunter, my old friend. Dean
Acheson said something to me that other day: 'Britain has
lost an Empire and not yet found a new role in the world.'

A beat.

MACMILLAN. We will have a fully functioning hydrogen
bomb within months.

EISENHOWER. Well, you may only have months. We are
going to push for a nuclear-test-ban treaty with the Soviets.

MACMILLAN. A test ban.

EISENHOWER. Oh yes. It's unthinkable that Britain wouldn't
sign too.

MACMILLAN. Yes.

EISENHOWER. Let off a big one and we'll talk again. But
make it the full orgasm.

He smiles. Yawns.

I think I'll turn in. I, er, hope you don't think I've kicked you
around a bit here. The bond we have won't break.

MACMILLAN. No.

EISENHOWER. Hey, let's have a breakfast party tomorrow. In pyjamas, why not – a pyjama party! The full British breakfast, like Montgomery used to serve up in North Africa.

MACMILLAN. Wonderful idea.

EISENHOWER. Goodnight, Harold.

MACMILLAN. Goodnight, Dwight.

EISENHOWER *exits.*

The scene is shifting to 10 Downing Street.

YOUNG MAC. 'Role in the world.'

MACMILLAN. I don't need you. All my life, I... Now I can be free of you. Go!

YOUNG MAC. Oh, please, Prime Minister, sir, I'll sit under the Cabinet Table, when you're discussing high affairs of state, you'll only hear a little snuffle now and then...

MACMILLAN *turns angrily on* YOUNG MAC, *his fist raised to strike him.* YOUNG MAC *falls back, looking up at* MACMILLAN.

Don't you know? If men don't carry their death inside them, they can't live.

He scuttles away on all fours and exits.

MACMILLAN *takes out cards and a small fountain pen. He makes emendations.*

MACMILLAN. Britain's role... 'The pattern of the Commonwealth is changing and with it Britain's position as the mother country. A wind of change is blowing through Africa...' 'Wind of change...' That's rather good. Won't waste it on Bradford.

Looks at a new card.

CROOKSHANK *enters quickly, a paper in his hand. Seeing* MACMILLAN *working, he stops.*

'And at home, you see prosperity such as we have never had in my lifetime. Britain has never been so good...'

Writes.

No...

CROOKSHANK. The Bradford speech?

MACMILLAN. Yes.

CROOKSHANK. How did Winston speak off-the-cuff so brilliantly?

MACMILLAN. He didn't.

CROOKSHANK. No?

MACMILLAN. Hours before the mirror. Being genuine in politics is all down to technique.

CROOKSHANK. Depressing.

MACMILLAN. I find it rather bracing. The great show of public life.

CROOKSHANK. Harold, Hugh Gaitskell just said that if Labour wins the election, they won't raise taxes.

A beat.

MACMILLAN. That's a mistake.

CROOKSHANK. Yes. People won't think he's genuine.

CROOKSHANK *exits.*

MACMILLAN *looks down at his notes.*

MACMILLAN. 'Go around the country...

He puts the notes away. He braces himself. As at a public meeting, addressing a big hall.

... go to the industrial towns, go to the farms and you will see prosperity such as we have never had in my lifetime – nor indeed in the history of this country. Britain has never been in such a good state. Indeed let us be frank about it: most of our people have never had it so good.'

The stage floods with the STAFF *of 10 Downing Street,*
CROOKSHANK *and* DOROTHY *with them. Champagne*
flows.

CROOKSHANK *raises his glass.*

CROOKSHANK. Conservatives, three hundred and sixty-five
seats. Labour, two hundred and fifty-five. Liberals, six. Inde-
pendents, one. A majority of one hundred and three. The
Prime Minister!

ALL. The Prime Minister!

MACMILLAN. Thank you. Now, to work!

They all exit except DOROTHY.

DOROTHY. You can do anything you want.

MACMILLAN. Yes, I can.

They stare at each other, then exit, separately.

Evening. Garden of the Château de Rambouillet, December
1962.

Enter SECURITY MEN *with weapons. They look around*
the stage.

YOUNG MAC *enters. He skulks around.*

MACMILLAN *enters. The* SECURITY MEN *scatter. He has*
an overcoat round his shoulders. He is smoking a cigarette.

YOUNG MAC. December 17th, 1962. Garden of the Château
de Rambouillet, La France. General de Gaulle, la la la.

MACMILLAN *turns.* YOUNG MAC *scuttles to the back of*
the stage.

Enter, also in evening dress, CROOKSHANK *and* LLOYD.
They have coats over their shoulders.

LLOYD. Absolutely bloody impossible.

CROOKSHANK. Does he understand a word we say?

MACMILLAN. Oh, he understands, he just doesn't choose to
reply.

LLOYD. Repeats himself again and again. '*La Republique, La Republique…*'

YOUNG MAC. La la la.

CROOKSHANK. I knew at the pheasant shoot it was going to go wrong. He seemed to have half the French Army as beaters, then didn't condescend to shoot a single bird himself. Just stood there criticising us when we missed.

LLOYD. Still, you did very well, Harold. What was it?

MACMILLAN. Seventy-seven out of a bag of three hundred and eighty-five.

LLOYD. You'd have thought that would have impressed him.

MACMILLAN. Where's Ted Heath?

CROOKSHANK. Still in his smoke-filled room with the French officials.

YOUNG MAC. '*Non.*'

CROOKSHANK. De Gaulle's going to say no, isn't he?

LLOYD. That is inconceivable.

YOUNG MAC. '*Le grand dessein. Non.*'

CROOKSHANK. The problem is nuclear. He's worried that our bomb is bigger than his. And that we show ours to the Americans.

LLOYD. We're like schoolboys, boasting about each other's willies.

MACMILLAN. Yes, and ours is bigger than his.

DOROTHY *enters in a very elegant coat.*

DOROTHY. I thought you'd be out here. What are you all doing?

MACMILLAN. Oh, boy's talk.

DOROTHY. I've slipped away from Madame de Gaulle. She has been showing me her very fine collection of lace. French lace. It's going wrong, isn't it?

MACMILLAN. No, it's fine.

DOROTHY. If de Gaulle won't agree, you can't fly to see Jack Kennedy next week. It'll make you look horribly weak. Eisenhower knew what a cantankerous old bastard de Gaulle is, but Kennedy doesn't carry that baggage.

MACMILLAN. I said, 'It's fine.'

A beat.

Then DOROTHY *turns and exits.*

LLOYD. Dorothy is right.

MACMILLAN (*to* CROOKSHANK). Get a message in to Ted. Tell him to carry on talking. And Selwyn, telex Washington. Give them the impression that Britain will be in Europe by the end of the year.

LLOYD. The French will be telling them the opposite.

MACMILLAN. But not in English.

LLOYD. No.

He hesitates. Then he exits hurriedly.

MACMILLAN. De Gaulle's always been a lost cause to any rational thought. And Kennedy... it's not the same as with Eisenhower.

CROOKSHANK. Kennedy fought in the war.

MACMILLAN. Yes, but there's no warmth. We photograph wonderfully well together, old statesman, young statesman... but there's nothing there, not really. I think, after all, Suez did sink us.

YOUNG MAC. Gamul Gamul Gamul.

MACMILLAN. It's not unravelling, is it, Harry? So quickly? The whole of my premiership...

CROOKSHANK. Harold, stop thinking like this. You won an election after a national catastrophe. You're hugely popular in the country.

MACMILLAN. Yes, yes, the *Daily Express* calls me 'Supermac'. That must mean something, mustn't it?

They exit.

Enter the DANCERS. *They dance to John Lennon's recording of 'Twist and Shout'.*

They finish the dance and exit.

10 Downing Street.

Enter MACMILLAN. *He is reading a copy of the* Daily Express *and is agitated.*

YOUNG MAC *sits at the back.*

Enter CROOKSHANK.

This freezing weather. The Board of Trade sent over figures showing it's driving up unemployment horribly.

CROOKSHANK. Well, I'm afraid it's set in.

MACMILLAN. A touch of frost and the country grinds to a halt.

CROOKSHANK. Harold...

MACMILLAN (*as if looking down out of a window*). We should do something about the garden come the spring.

CROOKSHANK. Yes, it's gone to pieces since Clemmie Churchill. Harold... General de Gaulle has made a broadcast on French national television. He has said 'no' to British entry.

A beat.

MACMILLAN. After all these months? 'No', and on television?

CROOKSHANK. It is an insult.

MACMILLAN. It's an age for insults. I went to the theatre last night.

CROOKSHANK. Yes?

MACMILLAN. A tacky little satire. Small theatre, packed out. It's all the rage.

CROOKSHANK. Harold, you didn't go and see *Beyond the Fringe*? Dear God, what were you thinking of?

MACMILLAN. I was thinking, show them that I'm a good
sport and can take a joke. Be 'with it'.

CROOKSHANK. Have the press got hold of this?

MACMILLAN. Not yet. No doubt they will.

CROOKSHANK. So... what did you think of the show?

MACMILLAN. There was a little shit called Peter Cook. He
was taking me off. It was mildly amusing...

YOUNG MAC *springs forward as Peter Cook doing his
'Macmillan'.*

YOUNG MAC. 'Now we shall receive four minutes' warning of
any impending nuclear attack. Some people have said, "Oh
my goodness me – four minutes? – that is not a very long
time!" Well, I would remind those doubters that some people
in this great country of ours can run a mile in four minutes.'

MACMILLAN. Then he saw me and... ad libbed.

CROOKSHANK. Ad libbed what?

YOUNG MAC *as Peter Cook again.*

YOUNG MAC. 'When I've a spare evening, there's nothing I
like better than to wander over to a theatre and sit there listening to a group of sappy, urgent, vibrant young satirists,
with a stupid great grin spread all over my silly old face.'

MACMILLAN. I was two rows from the front. I had to.

CROOKSHANK. Had to what?

MACMILLAN. Grin. I think I am the only Prime Minister in
history who has ever been publicly insulted to his face. I had
MI5 send round Cook's file. Nothing much: beastly to a few
women, a bit of a drink problem. What does this toerag of a
third-rate university comedian know? He has no conception
of what you and I, by the time we were his age, had suffered,
what demons within we had battered down! Did millions die
for a worthless young drunk, called Peter Cook, to stand on a
tatty stage and piss on their graves?

CROOKSHANK. Actually, I think he's rather talented.

MACMILLAN. You've been?

CROOKSHANK. 'Fraid so.

MACMILLAN. Along with many others, no doubt.

CROOKSHANK. It's froth.

MACMILLAN. Age of insults and froth.

A beat.

I suppose I should say, well, we won them freedom. The democratic right to booze and jokes. To be angry about nothing much... just angry about being angry. The freedom to fritter freedom away. No, I'm damned if I'd say that! There was something else, you said there was something else...

CROOKSHANK. Yes. It's one of your ministers. I'm afraid he may have got... entangled with a girl.

MACMILLAN. 'Entangled'?

CROOKSHANK. She's some kind of prostitute.

MACMILLAN. Well, at least it's girls this time, not boys. Who is it?

CROOKSHANK. Jack Profumo.

MACMILLAN. Well, we all know Jack's a randy fellow. Is this going to take up the rest of the day?

CROOKSHANK. The thing is... MI5 say the girl's also sleeping with a diplomat at the Russian Embassy.

A beat.

Jack's waiting in your study.

MACMILLAN. Down, down I come, like fallen Lucifer.

CROOKSHANK *exits.*

Downing Street, a month later. Whisky decanter, glasses on a small table. A copy of the Daily Express *upon it.*
MACMILLAN *picks it up and reads it, pacing, shaking the paper from time to time in an irritated way.*

Enter BOOTHBY.

Ah. Bob.

BOOTHBY. Prime Minister.

MACMILLAN. Scotch?

BOOTHBY. Yes please.

MACMILLAN *pours them both a drink, the Express under his arm. They drink, looking at each other.*

MACMILLAN. You said you'd be loyal.

BOOTHBY. I am.

MACMILLAN. I had to pass you over.

BOOTHBY. Yes.

MACMILLAN. And... there was personal spite.

BOOTHBY. Yes.

MACMILLAN. But we spent years together with Winston in the wilderness, I hope that still counts?

BOOTHBY. Yes, of course, Harold.

MACMILLAN. I need your help.

BOOTHBY. Anything.

MACMILLAN. My problem is... I don't understand the time we're living in. Look at this! A photograph of Jack Profumo in the *Express*. My Minister of War is pictured bouncing up and down on a bed.

BOOTHBY. He was visiting barracks at Aldershot. I suppose he wanted to show that army beds are... well-sprung.

MACMILLAN. But the photograph is next to yet another story about the Christine Keeler girl. Something about a West Indian boxer in Notting Hill. Prostitute, minister, prostitute, minister, day after day...

BOOTHBY. Isn't Jack's denial watertight? He stood up in Parliament and said he didn't sleep with the girl, full stop.

MACMILLAN. These days, I fear, a denial in Parliament is seen as an outright confession.

BOOTHBY. You slapped him on the back and said 'well done'. Of course, everyone knows Jack did sleep with her.

MACMILLAN. Jack denied it...

BOOTHBY. Surely MI5...

MACMILLAN. He denied it to my face!

BOOTHBY. Does that make a difference?

MACMILLAN. He commanded the 15th Army Group in Italy. Got the military OBE.

BOOTHBY. That is the difference?

MACMILLAN. Yes.

He loses his temper.

Dear God, why can't people keep their bodies under control? You know this world, Bob: osteopaths and Notting Hill gunmen, clubs, parties with masked men. Why are people so obsessed with it?

BOOTHBY. It's freedom, Harold.

MACMILLAN. Freedom's about building a better world.

BOOTHBY. It's about being and doing whatever you want.

MACMILLAN. We didn't win the war so people could indulge themselves!

BOOTHBY. A nude girl stepping out of a swimming pool, to embrace a middle-aged minister. Jack Profumo's story, it speaks to people. It has a kind of beauty, a dream of power and desire.

MACMILLAN. I do not understand.

BOOTHBY. I'm a rake, I know. You're a moral man, worth ten, a hundred of me. But in a way I'm real, you're not. All your public-service spirit, self-denial... your paternal Tory notion of helping people improve themselves... It's shit. Shit,

Harold. It's the sixties, the country's at peace. People don't want self-discipline, self-restraint, they want pleasure. The self. The gratification of the self. And lots of it.

MACMILLAN. What are you saying? Sex parties are a democratic right?

BOOTHBY. Absolutely.

MACMILLAN. This kind of thing could make the country ungovernable!

BOOTHBY. It's going, Harold. Deference, respect. And a bloody good thing too.

MACMILLAN. We've got a duty, a duty to each other, to what Britain can be.

BOOTHBY. Harold, no one cares.

MACMILLAN. So what is your advice, to a moral but out-of-touch Prime Minister?

BOOTHBY. Perhaps morally deficient times need a new kind of leader.

MACMILLAN. Who is also morally deficient.

BOOTHBY. Why not?

A beat.

MACMILLAN. Thank you, Bob.

They look at each other.

BOOTHBY *exits.*

The garden of 10 Downing Street. Snow falls.

MACMILLAN, *wrapped up, slumps on a garden seat.* YOUNG MAC *joins him, sitting by his side, his head on his lap.* MACMILLAN *strokes his hair.*

DOROTHY *enters.*

DOROTHY. Did you have an inkling Jack had lied to Parliament?

MACMILLAN. Oh yes.

DOROTHY. You knew from the start.

MACMILLAN. Yes.

DOROTHY. You were right to try to protect him. People shouldn't be pulled down like that.

MACMILLAN. No, one should rally round adulterers.

A beat.

DOROTHY. Well, now you can carry on.

MACMILLAN. No.

DOROTHY. The scandal's over. People forget.

MACMILLAN. No. It's the ridicule. It has reached what I believe atom scientists call 'a critical mass'. I am about to turn into a political mushroom cloud. Scattering a rather large amount of fallout over the Conservative Party, I'm afraid.

DOROTHY. You can't give up.

MACMILLAN. 'It's' no longer there.

DOROTHY. 'It'?

MACMILLAN. I'm going to resign.

DOROTHY. No.

MACMILLAN. I think ill health. Yes, I can work on 'ill health'. Something the public of this decade will understand. Cancerous, perhaps.

DOROTHY. I won't let them destroy you.

MACMILLAN. Well, you've been trying to do the job for years, my love.

DOROTHY. Harold, you are the most precious thing in my life.

MACMILLAN. Don't mock. I hate it when you mock...

DOROTHY. You are my true love.

MACMILLAN *scoffs.*

MACMILLAN. I think roly-poly Bob has that job. He told me he's a rake, straight out. It's a wonder over all these years you've not found yourself dis... diseased...

MACMILLAN *weeps*.

DOROTHY. He's like... a bad place I have to go to. I don't know why. But really, it's always been you. To me, you are everything that's good.

MACMILLAN. I sent forty-thousand Russian prisoners of war back to the Soviet Union. Stalin killed them all.

DOROTHY. You had no choice.

MACMILLAN. There is always a choice. The nuclear accident at the Windscale reactor. We needed it to make the British bomb. I ordered a cover-up, brave people who put the reactor's fire out were blamed.

DOROTHY. But the Americans shared their secrets with us because we had the bomb. You did it for Britain.

MACMILLAN. Eton. At Eton. I fell in love with a boy, a fellow Colleger, two years older than me. I betrayed him. He was ruined, I was taken away.

DOROTHY. I know.

MACMILLAN. You know?

DOROTHY. Your mother told me.

MACMILLAN. When?

DOROTHY. Just before we got married.

MACMILLAN. Ah.

DOROTHY. He was a sexual predator, Harold. You were an innocent.

MACMILLAN. None of us is innocent.

DOROTHY. Still got that bit of Catholic in you, haven't you, my dear?

MACMILLAN. We must all be judged. By God or by history. I doubt whether either will be kind to me.

DOROTHY *looks at her watch.*

What is it? Drinks with Bob at the Ritz?

DOROTHY. No.

MACMILLAN. Go.

DOROTHY. I...

MACMILLAN. I'll see you later this evening.

DOROTHY. Yes.

She kisses his head and exits.

YOUNG MAC *kneels beside* MACMILLAN, *who stands and, in his 'relaxed old man' mode, addresses the audience.*

MACMILLAN. A few months later, talked myself into prostate cancer and out of Number Ten. Then out of the cancer. And into a statesmanlike old fartdom. Which I rather enjoyed. I wrote my autobiography, at enormous length, five volumes, all remaindered long ago. You can, though, Google an American bookseller called AbeBooks and pick them up for next to nothing. My life. My life. Tarnished silver, perhaps, but solid. British. With a genuine hallmark: 'Democratic politician.'

A beat.

Thank you all very much and good evening.

The End.